HOW THINGS WORK

The Human Body, Plants, Animals, Seasons, Electricity, Computers, Smartphones, Flight, Architecture, Recycling, and More!

JAMIE THORNE

ISBN: 978-1-962481-06-9

FREE BONUS

SCAN TO GET OUR NEXT BOOK FOR FREE!

TABLE OF CONTENTS

INTRODUCTION

How do aircraft stay up in the air and not drop? Why will a car sink when it falls into the water, but a ship more than twice its size stays floating without sinking? How about elevators? What pulls them up and slides them down when you press a small button?

These questions are, well... they're only natural. Perhaps even more accurately, it's only *human*. Although curiosity apparently killed the cat, we're confident enough to guarantee that this book won't kill you (and yes, we checked with our legal team before making this statement!) So go ahead, let your guard down a bit, cozy up on the couch, a chair, or in your bed, and get ready to learn — *how things work!*

HOW THINGS WORK is a curiosity-quenching guide that dives into the many marvels, both natural and manmade. Humans have been able to create amazing things by thinking outside the box; thanks to human ingenuity, you now get to board a train, keep your milk in the refrigerator, use a cell phone, and do all sorts of other fascinatingly mundane things. However, we assure you that these things were once considered far from mundane!

As you flip through the pages of each chapter, you will learn about things like boats, the human body, engines, aircraft, bridges, forklifts, electricity, seasons, and weather. Apart from these, you will learn about 26 other fascinating things.

By the time your curiosity has flowed through each of the fascinating chapters of this book, you will have learned how these things work, the major parts that make them usable and useful for the world, and some even more amazing facts about them.

Prepare your mind and brace yourself as you are about to go on an unforgettable exploration into the air, land, and sea. So, grab a pen and some paper (or maybe something a bit more waterproof!), and let's dive into each of these wonders of the world.

CHAPTER ONE:
THE HUMAN BODY

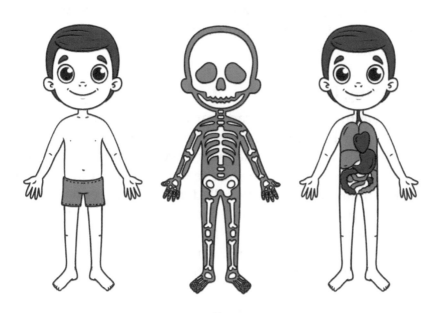

Your body is a fascinating machine, one with many parts, many of which you would never guess existed! From your head to your toes and everything in between, there are some pretty amazing little components. Let's dive in and learn a bit about how things work.

Bones: Your Internal Framework

Let's start with the bones! They are the strong framework of your body. They give you shape and power and protect parts of your body known as *organs*, from your heart to your kidneys. Your bones are like a nearly impenetrable castle. Just like bricks hold up a house, your bones support the great structure that is your body.

Muscles: The Body's Movers

Next up, let's talk about muscles. Muscles are organic engines that enable you to move your body. Think about muscles as powerful rubber bands that are attached to your bones. When you need to move, your brain sends signals to these "rubber bands" to tighten or relax. It's sort of like pulling a puppet's strings, except your brain is the one in control. Because muscles act in pairs, when one pulls, the other relaxes, allowing your arms, legs, and even your smile to do their work.

The Amazing Brain

Now, let's venture into the headquarters or command station of your body: your brain. It's like a supercomputer that never stops working, even when you're sleeping. Everything you do—from walking and talking to thinking and feeling—is controlled by your brain. It has billions of little cells called *neurons* that send messages to various parts of your body. They do this through a large network known as *the nervous system*. The next time you solve a puzzle or learn something new, remember that the command center that is your brain is calling all the shots.

Heart and Circulatory System

There's a real-life superhero inside your body: your heart. Your heart functions as a pump that circulates blood throughout your body, and your blood, like a delivery truck, delivers nutrients and oxygen to every part of your body. Without the hard work of your heart, the rest of your body could not function. The circulatory system is like a system of highways that allow your blood to flow throughout all of your body, nourishing your cells. Your heart beats around 100,000 times daily, pumping blood to fuel your body and keep you thriving.

Breath of Life

Take a deep breath. Feel that full feeling in your lungs? Your respiratory system brings oxygen into your body, removing waste gasses such as carbon dioxide. It's similar to a super-charged AC system at a hotel, always cranked up as powerfully as you'd like it to be. Air enters your lungs through your nose or mouth, down your windpipe, and into your lungs as you inhale. There, oxygen enters your bloodstream, where it provides energy for all your body's actions. A deep breath or two is always a surefire way to help you feel more energized and ready to go!

Digestive System and Nutrients

Let's move on to the marvelous digestive system. It's like a food handling and processing facility inside you. When you eat, your body uses your teeth and saliva to break down the food into smaller bits. The food then passes through your esophagus and into your stomach, where it is further broken down. Food nutrients are absorbed into your bloodstream and used to fuel your body.

Senses and Communication

Now, let's explore your incredible senses. Your five senses are those that help you see, hear, taste, smell, and touch. Your eyes capture the beautiful world around you, and your ears pick up on music and laughter. Your taste buds delight in tasty treats, your nose senses the pleasant perfume of flowers or the aroma of freshly baked cookies, and your skin helps you feel gentle touches, sharp pains, and everything in between. These senses allow us to interact with the world, people, plants, household objects, and all the other things on this incredible planet of ours.

Immune System, the Protector

Your body has a powerful defender called *the immune system*. It's like an army of tiny soldiers guarding you against harmful invaders. Your immune system is the shield that protects you from germs and keeps you from getting sick. White blood cells are the superheroes of your immune system, fighting off viruses and bacteria. They work hard to keep you strong and ward off any unwelcome "guests."

GROWTH AND DEVELOPMENT

As you grow older, your body goes through incredible changes. You start life as an infant and grow into a strong, capable adult. Your bones lengthen, your muscles strengthen, and you grow taller. It's a miraculous transformation, and your body is the vehicle that transports you through it. It's a wild and often dizzying ride but knowing a bit more about the process is always a great way to make things at least a *little* less wild.

All of this is only the beginning of the adventure of learning how your amazing body works; there's still so much curiosity left to satisfy! Always follow your curiosity, ask a few questions, and keep marveling at the incredible world within. After all, the world's smartest people are still learning new facts about the human body every single day. Our bodies are truly remarkable machines, and understanding how they work helps us to take care of them and keep them running smoothly.

Are you ready for the next adventure? Let's dive in for another swim through the seas of curiosity.

CHAPTER TWO:
PLANTS

Our curious journey now arrives in the enchanting world of plants.

Have you ever wondered how those beautiful flowers bloom or how trees grow tall and strong? Prepare to embark on a lean, mean, and *green* adventure as we dive into the fascinating workings of plants. Keep reading to uncover the secrets of the botanical world, from small seeds to towering trees.

Seeds

Nature's Magic Packages: Seeds are like nature's magic packages. They include all the instructions and information needed to start a new plant. Think of a seed as a "jack-in-the-box" toy waiting for the right moment to pop up from beneath the soil. Once a seed is planted into fertile soil and watered, it sprouts and grows out its roots, stems, and leaves.

Roots

Nature's Anchors: Imagine going on a treasure hunt and discovering a hidden chest filled with precious gems. Well, roots can be seen as types of "treasure hunters" searching for jewels of precious water to nourish the rest of the plant. They anchor plants into the ground, keeping them stable and secure. Roots also function similarly to straws, sucking water and nutrients from the soil and passing them up to the plant. Plants require water to survive and flourish, just as you do to quench your thirst and keep on living it up.

Stems

Nature's Superhighways: Have you ever noticed the tall, sturdy parts that flowers attach to or the thick trunks of trees? Stems are like nature's superhighways, transporting water, nutrients, and food from the roots all throughout the plant. They also act as support beams, holding up leaves, flowers, and fruits. Next time you see a beautiful bouquet of roses or a towering tree, remember that stems play a vital role in keeping plants alive and thriving.

Leaves

Nature's Solar Panels: Plant leaves are nature's very own solar panels; they absorb sunlight and convert it into energy. Leaves come in various forms and sizes, as well as different textures. There are tiny holes in the leaves that help plants breathe by taking in carbon dioxide and releasing oxygen. So, when you take a deep breath of fresh air, don't forget to thank your lucky star-... uh ... lucky *trees*.

Flowers

Nature's Colorful Artworks: Ah, flowers, one of mother nature's finest masterpieces. Flowers can be truly dazzling works of art. They come in an incredible variety of colors, forms, and smells, but did you realize that flowers actually serve a pretty big purpose in addition to looking pretty? They attract pollinators such as bees, butterflies, and birds. It's as though the plant is throwing a grand party, with nectar as a delicious treat. When pollinators visit flowers, they help transfer pollen from one flower to another, allowing plants to produce seeds and continue their life cycle.

Plant Reproduction

Ensuring Survival: Plants have a clever way of reproducing to ensure survival. While flowers play a part in attracting pollinators, they also produce fruits. Fruits are like nature's little packages that the plant produces to protect its seeds. When an animal eats a fruit or it falls to the ground, the seeds inside are dispersed. Some may find a new spot to grow, creating new plants. This is a plant's way of spreading its family across the land.

THE POWER OF PHOTOSYNTHESIS

Plants have a special power called photosynthesis. Just as you need food to grow and stay healthy, plants need something special, too: sunlight! Leaves act as solar panels, absorbing the sun's energy.

The plant then converts sunlight, water, and carbon dioxide into food with the help of a very efficient chemical known as *chlorophyll*. It's like having a built-in kitchen that makes delicious meals.

ADAPTING TO THE ENVIRONMENT

Plants are incredible survivors and have adapted to different environments and climates all over the planet. Some plants thrive in deserts, others in rainforests, and some even in depths of the sea. They have unique features, like thick, waxy coatings, spines, or the ability to store water. These adaptations help them survive and thrive in their specific habitats.

EXPLORING THE WONDERS OF PLANTS

Plant Crafts and Art: Plants offer a world of creativity and inspiration. You can create beautiful artwork using leaves, flowers, and stems. Pressing flowers and leaves between the pages of a book can preserve their beauty and make them perfect for crafting. You can also make leaf rubbings by placing a leaf below a piece of paper and gently rubbing a colored pencil or crayon over it. You can get creative with things and let your imagination blossom.

Gardening adventures: Do you have a green thumb? Gardening is a fantastic way to connect with plants and learn more about their needs. You can plant your flower or vegetable garden and watch your plants grow from seeds to full-fledged wonders. Discover the joy of nurturing plants, watering them, and watching them thrive. Plus, you can enjoy the satisfaction of harvesting your own fresh produce!

Nature walks and plant identification: Embark on exciting nature walks to explore the plant kingdom around you. Take a notebook or a field guide with you to identify the different types of plants you encounter. Look for unique leaf shapes, vibrant flowers, or exciting bark patterns. You can even create a plant scavenger hunt by listing specific plants to find. It's like being a plant detective!

By this point, you've become budding botanists. You've explored the incredible world of plants, from their inner workings to the fantastic things we can do with them. Plants are not just beautiful and fascinating; they offer us endless opportunities for creativity, discovery, and enjoyment. So, feel free to embrace the wonders of plants and let their magic inspire you in your everyday life.

CHAPTER THREE:
ANIMALS

Welcome to the next adventure: exploring the captivating world of animals. From the tiniest insects in your garden to the mightiest creatures of the African savanna, animals are the incredible beings that inhabit our planet. Prepare to embark on an exciting animal expedition as we uncover the secrets of their fascinating lives. Come along on this wild ride filled with fun facts, unique adaptations, and unusual behaviors.

CLASSIFICATION OF ANIMALS

Animals come in various shapes, sizes, and types. We can classify them into different groups based on their similarities. Let's explore some of the major groups of animals:

Mammals: Mammals are animals with fur or hair that give live birth to their young ones (instead of laying eggs) and nurse them with milk. Mammals exhibit diverse behaviors and adaptations, from affectionate dogs and cats to majestic elephants and playful dolphins.

Birds: Birds are best known for their ability to fly, although not every bird can actually fly; penguins, for example, can't fly. They have feathers, lay eggs, and possess remarkable beaks and wings. From colorful and talkative parrots to graceful eagles and adorable hummingbirds, birds showcase an array of shapes and sizes. Some birds are also pretty amazing singers!

Reptiles: Reptiles are cold-blooded animals (meaning their bodies can't regulate their own temperature) with scales—some, like turtles, even have shells! They lay eggs and often have unique adaptations that allow them to survive in different habitats. Animals in this group often move or crawl low to the ground. Snakes, turtles, lizards, and crocodiles are some examples of reptiles that roam our planet. Some of these animals have beautiful skin with artistic patterns on them.

Amphibians: Amphibians are fascinating animals that can live on both land and water. Most begin their life in the water as tadpoles before developing into adults; at this point, most move onto land. Some of the amphibians that capture us with their amazing life cycles are frogs, toads, and salamanders.

Fish: Fish are animals that live exclusively in water. They have organs called *gills that extract oxygen from water, allowing them to breathe.* From colorful saltwater fish living in coral reefs to the deep sea's stealthy sharks and unique seahorses, fish come in all sorts of colors and patterns. Some varieties of small fish make good pets, too, like Oscar, Barb, Tiger Barb, and Blue Tang, among others.

Arthropods: With millions of species, arthropods are the most diverse group of animals on the planet. This classification includes insects, which have six legs, three body sections, and sometimes wings. Also included are arachnids, such as spiders and ticks, and crustaceans, like crabs and lobsters. Arthropods are essential to the environment, from buzzing bees and beautiful butterflies to scuttling crabs and web-spinning spiders.

HOW ANIMALS ADAPT

Animals have remarkable adaptations that help them survive in their environments. Let's look at some fascinating adaptations that make animals unique:

Camouflage: Many animals develop camouflage, which helps them blend into their surroundings. From the stripes of a tiger to the color-changing abilities of a chameleon, camouflage is a remarkable adaptation for hunting or, conversely, avoiding predators.

Mimicry: Some animals have the incredible ability to mimic other species. This can serve as a defense mechanism or a way to trick prey. For instance, the venomous coral snake is mimicked by the harmless scarlet king snake to ward off predators.

Protective Armor: Certain animals have evolved protective armor to shield themselves from danger. Think of an armadillo or pangolin's armored plates or a turtle's tough shell. These adaptations help them survive in challenging environments.

Specialized Body Parts: Animals have developed specialized body parts to suit their unique lifestyles. From the long neck of a giraffe to the strong beak of a woodpecker, these adaptations enable animals to find food, build nests, or defend themselves.

Echolocation: Some animals, such as bats and dolphins, have echolocation skills to navigate and locate objects in their environment; they generate sounds and listen for echoes. It's like having a built-in sonar system!

Migration: Many animals travel long distances to acquire food, breed, or escape bad weather. Migration is an exciting adaptation that demonstrates the endurance and determination of animals. Many different types of animals migrate, from the magnificent monarch butterfly to enormous humpback whales.

HOW DO ANIMALS COMMUNICATE?

Animals communicate with each other using many various methods. While they may not use words like we humans do, their signals and, often, even *behaviors* convey important messages. Let's explore some fascinating ways animals communicate:

Vocalizations: Like humans, many animals, such as birds, whales, and monkeys, use vocalizations to communicate. They create unique sounds, songs, or calls to express their intentions, mark territories, or attract mates.

Body language: Animals use body language to communicate various emotions and intentions. From wagging tails and fluffed feathers to threatening postures and displays, their movements and gestures convey messages to others.

Scent marking: Many animals use scent to inform others of their presence in the area or to attract mates; they release chemicals or leave smell imprints in their territory. Spraying skunks or scent-marking wolves are two examples of animals that use their scent.

Visual displays: Animals often use visual displays to communicate during mating or when fighting over territory. Animals can use their bright feathers, elaborate dances, and stylized postures to attract potential mates or establish dominance.

You've now made your way through an exciting safari into the world of animals. From their classification and adaptations to their unique communication methods, animals continue to amaze humans with their diversity and ingenuity. Remember to observe and respect the animals around you, for they are truly beings that inspire and amaze, helping the planet's various ecosystems along the way.

CHAPTER FOUR:
SEASONS

This chapter will be about seasons, which are super cool and, well, they're also super *hot, warm, cold,* and *everything* in between. You'll be taken on an exciting adventure to discover the fantastic world of seasons. Get ready to dig in and explore how the planet changes throughout the year, bringing different weather, fun activities, and beautiful sights.

WHAT ARE SEASONS?

Seasons are periods of time when the temperature changes, which impacts plant and animal life. Do you know how you change your clothes depending on whether it's hot or cold outside? The planet does something similar—but on a far larger scale. Earth experiences four distinct seasons: spring, summer, autumn (or fall), and winter. Seasons are the four periods of the year, marked by specific weather patterns and daylight hours. Each season has its own distinct characteristics that make it different from the other three.

Get ready to discover the mysteries of changing landscapes, weather patterns, and the numerous wonders that accompany each season.

Spring: Spring takes place from late March to late June in some places and late September to late December in other places. It is often seen as a period of rebirth after winter, with warmer temperatures, longer days, and increased plant growth and blooming. Imagine what waking up from a long, nice sleep feels like; this is how nature feels as winter gives way to spring. Flowers begin to blossom as the weather warms, turning parks and gardens into a riot of color. Birds return from their winter vacations and begin chirping cheerful songs. In many parts of the globe, it's the ideal weather for playing outside, spotting baby animals, and flying kites in the soft breeze.

Summer: Summer is another season distinguished by warm weather, long days, and sunshine. Summer is about having fun in the sun. The sun beams brightly, and the temperature rises. It's the season for outdoor adventures and nonstop entertainment, like swimming in cool lakes, making sandcastles on the beach, and having picnics in the park. The daylight hours are longer, providing you with more time to enjoy games, ride bikes, and explore nature.

Autumn: Autumn is a season of transition. This is the season that comes between summer and winter and is distinguished by colder temperatures, shorter days, and the fall of tree leaves. Also known as *fall* in North America, autumn is a period when many plants and trees drop their leaves in preparation for winter, and some animals begin to migrate to warmer locations. Autumn arrives when the days become shorter, and a slight chill infuses the air. It is also a season of incredible transformations; trees are adorned with blazing colors of red, orange, and gold, creating a colorful carpet of leaves that crunch beneath your feet as you walk through them. Autumn is harvest season for farmers when many fruits and vegetables ripen and are ready to be gathered. Don't forget the fun of jumping into leaf mounds! During this season, a lot of fun and exciting activities are available for you to enjoy, such as going on nature hikes, jumping in leaf piles, baking autumn goodies, or having a bonfire or backyard campfire (safely, of course!)

Winter: Winter is the season that follows autumn before giving way to the next spring. It is the coldest season of the year, with temperatures frequently dropping below freezing in some climates, and is commonly distinguished by snow and ice. Winter brings shorter days and longer nights, and many plants and animals adapt to the cold by going dormant. Some people like winter sports, such as skiing, snowboarding, and ice skating, while others prefer to stay indoors and warm up in front of a cozy fire. Winter comes with magnificent landscapes blanketed in a soft, white overflow of snow. It's the time of year for snowball battles, building snowmen, and sledding down snowy hills. Winter holidays, such as Christmas and Hanukkah, allow you to spend time with family, exchange gifts, and express love and joy. You may curl up by the fireplace, sip hot chocolate, and enjoy the company of your loved ones.

HOW DO
SEASONS CHANGE?

Have you ever thought about why we have various seasons? It's because of how our planet rotates around the sun. The Earth, you see, is slightly inclined, like a spinning top. Summer occurs when one portion of the Earth leans toward the sun. When that part of the Earth leans away, it becomes winter. The other two seasons happen when the Earth is not tilting too far in either direction. Understanding and appreciating the four seasons is an awesome adventure. Each season has its own distinct charm and beauty, offering humanity a constantly changing landscape and a wide range of experiences.

Now that you understand the four seasons, you can better enjoy the natural cycles and the beauty they provide. You will also be able to adjust to the changing weather conditions and enjoy the unique chances that each season offers. So, embrace the enchantment of winter, the warmth of summer, the beauty of fall, and the wonder of spring. For inquiring minds, the four seasons await, offering a world of inquiry and wonder.

CHAPTER FIVE:
WEATHER

Have you ever wondered why it's sunny one day and rainy the next? Why, for example, do you need a jacket in the winter but not in the summer? In this chapter, you will delve into the fascinating world of weather and discover the astounding mechanics that govern its operation.

WHAT IS WEATHER?

Weather is how the Earth expresses itself through the sky. The weather determines if it will be sunny, rainy, windy, snowy, or even stormy. Weather is the temporary state of the atmosphere, the layer of air that surrounds the Earth. Consider it Mother Nature's way of displaying her many faces. The weather varies from day to day and can differ in different places of the world.

TYPES OF WEATHER

Sunny: You can call the sun the strongest weather wizard, possessing the secret to all weather magic. When the sun shines, it illuminates and warms the globe. However, the interesting part is that the sun does not heat each part of the Earth equally; some areas receive more sunlight and heat than others. These uneven temperatures cause all sorts of weather adventures. Have you ever noticed how some days are hot while others are cold? This is due to temperature, which measures how warm or cold the air around you is. When the sun shines directly on something, it warms it up and makes it feel hotter. However, when the sun's rays strike at an angle, like in winter, it feels colder.

Windy: Wind is caused by the transfer of air from one location to another due to changes in temperature and air pressure. Wind is created when warm air rises and cool air rushes in to fill the gap. From a summer breeze to a powerful gust during a storm, we can feel all sorts of wind in all sorts of weather. The wind is a natural phenomenon that has captivated humanity for years, inspiring things like poetry and music. The wind significantly impacts the surroundings and your experiences, whether it's a moderate breeze or a forceful gale. The wind has an impact not just on recreational activities, such as flying a kite, but also on long-term attempts to build a greener future through the use of windmills. The wind is an amazing power with many different effects on people's lives.

Cloudy: Clouds look like fluffy blots of white or gray paint that decorate the sky. They are made up of tiny droplets of water or ice crystals floating in the air. Clouds come in different shapes and sizes, from puffy "cotton candy" clouds to dark stormy ones. When clouds get heavy enough with moisture, they release rain, snow, or even hail. However, as we all know, behind those rain clouds is a chance for a beautiful rainbow to appear.

Stormy: Sometimes, the weather gets really exciting and sometimes even scary! Lightning dances across the sky and thunder rumbles like a hungry giant's belly. Thunderstorms happen when powerful currents of warm and cold air clash, causing strong winds and rain. Lightning is caused by a rapid discharge of electricity between the ground and the clouds. One thing you may not know about lightning is that the flashes of light we see start at the ground and travel upward! It happens so quickly, though, that sometimes it looks like it's coming from the sky. You don't have to worry, though; storms can be fascinating and beautiful to watch as long as you stay safe indoors.

You have just explored the fascinating world of weather. Weather is an ever-changing journey that shapes the world, from the sun's warming beams to the playful wind, from fluffy clouds to thunderous storms. Keep looking up, asking questions, and marveling at the beauty of the sky. Every day, rain or shine offers new discoveries.

CHAPTER SIX: TIME

Have you ever wondered why some days seem to go by in a flash while others feel like they last forever? Or how it is that we can *measure* moments in hours and in days? We're about to embark on a fascinating journey as the secret of time is unraveled, so buckle up for an adventure through the ticking world of clocks and calendars.

WHAT IS TIME?

Time can be seen as a never-ending river that everyone swims through. Measuring time allows humans to organize and quantify their days, weeks, months, and years. Clocks are one of the tools we use to measure time; they tell you when to get out of bed, play, eat, and sleep. Clocks are one method of keeping track of your experiences and making sense of your surroundings.

We measure time so we can comprehend the passage of moments. Clocks and calendars enable you to determine when events occur and how long they last. Assume you have a unique clock that displays the hours and minutes. When the big and little hands move, you know time is passing. You use time to plan out your day. There is, for example, a specific time when you wake up in the morning. Then you have breakfast, shower, and go to school, all at various times. Over time, you learn when to do different things and can develop habits based on your own perception of time.

These time-measuring tools also help you understand the order of events. They can tell you if something happened in the past, is happening now, or will happen in the future. For example, yesterday means the day before today, and tomorrow means the day after today. The tools and language humans have developed to explain time help you keep track of these different moments. Basically, these special tools and words help you know when things happen, how long they last, and the order in which they happen. They are guides that help you navigate through your day and understand the world around you.

THE TICK-TOCK
OF CLOCKS

A clock is a unique device that allows you to measure the seconds, minutes, and hours in each day. It contains two important visual parts: the hour hand and the minute hand; some clocks even have a third hand for seconds. These hands travel in circles around the face of the clock. The hour hand is shorter and indicates which of the 12 hours of the day it is. The minute hand is longer and indicates how many minutes have gone by since the previous hour. It refers to the minute numbers on the clock, of which there are 60.

An hour has elapsed when the minute hand moves all the way around the clock and returns to the top, where you see the number 12. When you look at a clock, you can see where the hour and minute hands are pointing, and once you know how to read a clock, this informs you what time it is. It allows you to keep track of exactly when to wake up, eat meals, go to school, and do other things during the day. Clocks serve as timekeepers. They aid in the measurement of time. You have definitely seen a variety of clocks, ranging from traditional ones with hands to digital clocks with numbers that change.

Clocks contain specific gears and springs that allow them to tick. Each tick signifies a passing second. Clocks come in a variety of styles and sizes. Some are hung on the wall, some, like watches, are worn, and some are found on electronic devices like phones and tablets. However, they all serve the same purpose: to help you keep track of time.

FROM SECONDS TO
MINUTES TO HOURS

Time is divided into different units, much like the measuring cups and spoons you use when you cook. A second is the smallest unit, and it takes 60 seconds to form one minute. Can you count to 60 in your head? Great! Now, 60 minutes equals one hour. You can't do much more than blink in a second, but an hour is enough time to do a variety of things, such as play a game, read a book, or watch a movie.

DAYS, WEEKS, AND MONTHS

Now, let's take a look at longer timeframes. There are 24 hours in each day. As the Earth turns on its axis, you experience day and night. Did you know it takes the Earth approximately 24 hours to complete one rotation? Isn't that incredible? Day occurs when your side of the Earth is facing the sun, and it becomes night when the planet turns away from the sun.

The next unit of measurement we use is a *week*. A week is made up of seven days. As you probably already know, each day of the week is given a unique name – Sunday, Monday, Tuesday, Wednesday, Thursday, Friday, and Saturday. You can also divide weeks into weekdays—the days from Monday to Friday—and weekends—Saturday and Sunday. Most schools hold classes on weekdays and take weekends off.

Months come next. There are 12 months, made up of about four weeks each. Each month has a unique name, such as January, February, or March. Most months are actually a few days longer than four weeks, with 30 or 31 days. However, February is exactly four weeks long, which means it only has 28 days; even more interesting is that every four years, we have a *leap year*, in which the month of February has an extra day. It's like a special bonus for the calendar! All of these 12 months together make one *year*.

Calendars allow us to keep track of the days, weeks, and months of each year. We call each day on the calendar a date and assign several numbers to each date that help us keep track of when things happen. Each day is given a number according to when it occurs in a month, and each month is followed by a number that represents the year. Think of dates like an address; the year is like the city you live in, the month is the name of your street, and the day is your house number. It's a safe bet that you know what date your birthday falls on! Just like addresses tell you where to find a house; dates show you "where" an event, like your birthday, occurs in time.

As you travel through time, you can make memories, learn new things, and spend quality time with family and friends. Be sure to enjoy every passing second, make the most of every hour, and treasure the great gift of time.

You have explored the enthralling world of time, from the tick-tock of clocks to the turning pages of calendars. Remember that time is about more than just digits on a clock or a calendar; it's about making the most of every minute by exploring, learning, and experiencing moments that make wonderful memories. So, get out there, have fun, and cherish the ticking world of time.

CHAPTER SEVEN: ELECTRICITY

Electricity is a type of energy you cannot see, but it can be used to provide power to numerous items. Many of the items which you use daily, such as your light bulbs, televisions, and computers, are powered by electricity. It can appear to be magical when all those things suddenly start working, but they are powered by the very real movement of very real things known as *electrons*.

Picture a road with vehicles traveling on it. Just as cars and trucks move down a highway, electrons, in the form of electricity, move down a metal "string" that we call a *wire*. Wires function similarly to pipes, transporting electricity from one location to another. The wires we use are usually in the form of cords, made up of two or more wires inside a plastic sheath. Permanent cords, like the ones installed in the walls of your house, are referred to as cables.

Now, electricity doesn't just appear out of nowhere; humans have found ways to convert things into a form of energy that you can use. First, electricity is generated in a *power plant*. A power plant isn't a "plant" in the way that trees and flowers are; instead, it's more like a massive factory that humans developed to produce electricity. Power plants create electricity in several different ways, using a variety of energy sources. Some methods of creating electricity include burning coal and natural gas, collecting light from the sun, and building windmills to harness the energy of wind.

Once generated, electricity travels through large cables, known as *power lines*, to reach houses, schools, and other structures. These electric cables are typically either high in the sky or buried underground in places where people won't be harmed by the enormous amount of energy they carry.

When it reaches your home, electricity enters through a particular box called an *electrical panel*. It then flows through smaller wires to outlets and switches in other parts of the house. An electrical *circuit* is completed when a device, such as a lamp or a phone charger, is plugged into an outlet using a power cord. An electrical circuit is a loop that enables electricity to move from the power source to the device and power it up. When you flip a switch, it opens or shuts the circuit, allowing you to regulate the flow of electricity.

However, it is best to use extra caution when working with electricity because it can be dangerous. Too much video game time might "fry your brain," but too much electricity will fry your whole body! That is why you see warnings and signs about not sticking things into electrical outlets or touching exposed wires. Using things known as "outlet covers" keeps everybody safe. Electricity powers gadgets all over the globe, and it's always best to use it properly and carefully.

BENEFITS OF ELECTRICITY

Light and Heat. Lightbulbs are powered by electricity, allowing you to see and do things even when it is dark outside. Electricity also provides power to the devices we use to produce heat, helping you stay warm in cold weather.

Powering Appliances. Appliances like refrigerators, stoves, microwaves, and washing machines are all powered by electricity, making daily chores much easier and faster.

Communication and Entertainment. Electricity allows you to communicate, learn, and enjoy yourself by powering devices like televisions, laptops, smartphones, and tablets. You can watch movies, play games, and communicate with people worldwide over the internet.

Transportation. Electricity is also essential in powering electric cars and trains, making transportation more environmentally friendly and efficient. Some additional features, like power windows, also use electricity.

DANGERS OF ELECTRICITY

Electrical Shock. You can be electrocuted by touching exposed wires or inserting things into electrical outlets. Electrocution can result in burns, injury, or even death. That's why you should never touch electrical wires with your bare hands or insert anything besides a power plug into an outlet.

Electrical Fires. Electricity is a powerful force that can produce sparks and a lot of heat. If you aren't careful when you use electricity, you don't just risk electrocution; you also risk starting a fire! Electrical fires can be caused by many things, from using the wrong power source to old or faulty wiring; that's why it's so important to be cautious and follow instructions when using electronics.

Water and Electricity. Because water conducts electricity, keeping electrical devices far from sources of water, like sinks, bathtubs, and pools, is critical. Touching electrical items with wet hands or standing on a damp surface is never a good idea; just don't do it!

Climbing and Falling Hazards. Climbing on trees, poles, or other structures near power lines is extremely dangerous and should be avoided. You should never fly kites or play with long things near power lines, either, as these items can conduct electricity and cause accidents.

To stay safe around electricity, you should follow these guidelines:

Never touch electrical wires or outlets. You must prioritize your safety and avoid accessing electrical cables or outlets. If you or any of your friends or siblings touch an electrical source, seek emergency medical attention immediately.

Do not play with electrical cords or appliances. You must be taught about the potential hazards of electricity and understand the laws and restrictions for using electrical gadgets. Do not persist in playing with cables when grownups keep them out of your grasp.

Ask an adult for help when plugging or unplugging devices.

Stay away from power lines and electrical equipment.

Never use electrical devices near water. Always make sure your hands are dry when handling electrical equipment. Also, never use devices like hairdryers, radios, or any other electronic devices near sinks, bathtubs, or swimming pools.

Inform an adult if you see any damaged electrical cords or outlets.

Remember, electricity is a wonderful and helpful resource, but using it safely and responsibly is vital to avoid accidents or harm.

CHAPTER EIGHT:
BATTERIES

Have you ever wondered how some of your favorite gadgets can function without being plugged into a power source? This is because they rely on *batteries*. Batteries are small, portable devices that store energy in the form of electricity, which we learned about in chapter seven. They act as powerhouses, supplying the energy required to keep things running. Batteries offer energy to power things in the same way that food supplies energy to your body.

A battery contains various parts that work together to generate electricity. On the outside of the battery, positive and negative *electrodes*, identified by the + and - symbols, provide a path for electricity to travel from the electrolyte inside a battery into the device it's meant to power. An electrolyte is a unique material that transfers electrically-charged particles called ions between these two electrodes. You might've heard of electrolytes already from your sports coach or health teacher. Amazingly enough, the very same electrolytes that are in sports drinks are in batteries! Electrolytes help electricity to flow smoothly between the electrodes inside a battery.

A circuit is completed when you insert a battery into a device, such as a toy or remote control. As you learned in the previous chapter, a circuit is a channel through which electricity can flow. When the circuit is completed, power begins to flow from the battery to the device. As electricity flows, the energy stored in the battery reduces. Because of this, batteries eventually run out of power and "die," at which point they must be replaced or recharged.

Batteries vary in shape and size depending on the devices they power. You may have seen cylindrical (long and circular) batteries, such as AA or AAA batteries, or flat batteries, like the ones in your watch. Some batteries are "disposable," so you can use them until their energy runs out and then dispose of them properly. Other batteries are "rechargeable," which means they can be re-energized using a charger. Because rechargeable batteries don't have to be thrown away, they are better for the environment, as they generate less waste.

Some safety guidelines when working with batteries:

Always use the correct type and size of battery recommended for your device. You should not try to modify or tamper with battery components, and you should always ask for the assistance of an adult when replacing batteries.

Insert the batteries in the correct direction, following the positive (+) and negative (-) markings on both the battery and the device.

If a battery starts to leak or gets damaged, **do not touch it**.

Dispose of old batteries according to local regulations, as some batteries contain harmful chemicals. It is essential that you are aware of the rules for the recycling of batteries and make sure to follow them.

BENEFITS OF
BATTERIES

Portability. One of the most significant advantages of batteries is their portability. Because batteries contain energy, they allow you to utilize devices without being plugged into an electrical outlet. This means you can bring your favorite toys, gadgets, and flashlights everywhere.

Convenience. Batteries are an easy way to get power. They are simple to install in gadgets; once installed, the device can be utilized immediately. Unlike power outlets, batteries allow you to use items without being restricted to a particular location.

Versatility. Batteries are used in a wide range of everyday objects, from toys and remote controls to cameras and portable music players. They are available in various forms and sizes to accommodate various devices and may be obtained at various stores.

DISADVANTAGES
OF BATTERIES

Limited Energy. Batteries can only hold a certain amount of energy. The device consumes the power stored in the battery, which will ultimately run out. This means you must monitor battery life and be prepared with replacements or chargers.

Environmental Impact. Some batteries contain chemicals that, if not disposed of appropriately, can be detrimental to the environment. Batteries that are discarded can end up in landfills and potentially release dangerous compounds into the soil or water. This is why recycling batteries or following precise disposal standards is critical to reducing their environmental impact.

Cost. Batteries can be costly, especially if you are continually replacing disposable batteries. While rechargeable batteries can be used several times, the initial cost is frequently higher due to the necessity of a charger. Always examine the long-term costs of battery use and select the most cost-effective alternative.

Batteries supply portable power and enable the use of many devices. However, it's important to use batteries responsibly, recycle them wherever feasible, and be aware of their finite energy capacity and potential environmental impact.

CHAPTER NINE: SOUND WAVES

WARM AIR

COOL AIR

Noises are everywhere; from the moment you wake up to the moment your head hits the pillow, you are constantly surrounded by noise. But have you ever thought about *how* or *why* you can hear noises like music, people chatting, or even a bee buzzing? These sounds travel in the form of what we call a *sound wave*. Sound waves are invisible vibrations that flow through the air, water, and even solid objects. These waves are a type of energy that allows you to hear various sounds.

Invisible vibrations are produced in the form of a wave when a sound is made, such as music from an instrument or a person's voice. These vibrations move through the air in all directions. When you pick up a pebble and throw it into a settled pool, ripples form and spread out from where the stone landed in the water. Just as these water waves travel from one point and spread all over, sound waves also ripple through the air around you.

HOW WE HEAR SOUNDS

Sound waves cause your *eardrums* to vibrate when they reach your ears. The eardrum is a tiny layer of tissue inside your ears that detects these vibrations. The vibrations are then transmitted to your brain, and the brain translates these waves into sounds that you can identify.

Sound waves don't just travel through the air; they can flow through other materials as well. For example, if you place your ear on a door, you might be able to hear someone on the other side talking. Sound waves are passing right through the door and into your ear. Oddly enough, there is one place sound waves can't travel through—outer space. Simply put, there is not enough "stuff" in outer space for sound waves to travel through!

Volume refers to how loud or soft a sound is. Some sounds, such as fireworks, can be deafening, while others, like a whisper, are much quieter. A sound's *pitch* is connected to how high or low it sounds. A whistle, for example, is a high-pitched sound, but a tuba or a bass produces a low-pitched sound.

You use sound waves in your daily lives in various ways, from listening to music to talking with your friends. Sound waves are also used by doctors and scientists in medical imaging, a technique called ultrasound. Sound waves allow them to construct images of the insides of our bodies. You may have heard of an ultrasound before; it lets doctors see babies before they're even born! So, the next time you hear a noise, remember that it's the result of sound waves flowing through the air and reaching your eardrums.

THE IMPORTANCE OF
SOUND WAVES

Sound waves play an essential part in your lives. They allow you to talk with your friends, hear music, and paint a picture of your surroundings. Here are some of the reasons why sound waves are significant:

Communication. Sound waves allow you to communicate with others and understand what they are saying. When you speak, your vocal cords vibrate, producing sound waves that travel to the listener's ears. You wouldn't be able to have a conversation or listen to stories and jokes if sound waves didn't exist.

Music and Entertainment. Music and entertainment are built on sound waves. Musical instruments such as guitars, pianos, and drums generate diverse sound waves that combine to form melodies, harmonies, and rhythms. Sound waves allow you to enjoy movies, TV shows, and live performances by transmitting voices, sound effects, and music.

Environmental Awareness. Sound waves assist you in comprehending your surroundings. They allow you to distinguish and identify noises like a dog barking, birds tweeting, or a car honking. They offer critical information about your environment, such as warning sounds, alarms, and even the sound of approaching footsteps.

Safety and Communication Devices. Sound waves are crucial in devices that allow you to communicate with individuals who are far away, such as telephones, intercoms, and walkie-talkies. They also enable emergency services, such as fire alarms and sirens, to warn you when there is a threat. These devices communicate crucial messages and keep you secure by using sound waves.

Sound waves are all around you, improving your life in various ways. They connect you, allow you to enjoy music and pleasure, aid you in understanding your surroundings, and have even enabled significant technological developments. The next time you hear a sound, you'll know that the immense power of sound waves is helping the world become more vibrant and interactive.

Here are a few disadvantages of sound waves:

Noise Pollution. Noise pollution, which refers to excessive or unwanted sounds that can be disruptive or hazardous to human health and the environment, is transmitted by sound waves. For example, prolonged exposure to certain sounds, such as construction noise or loud music, can cause hearing impairment. Stress, sleep difficulties, and difficulty concentrating can all be caused by noise pollution.

Interference and Distortion. Interference and distortion can occur when sound waves move across complicated surroundings or encounter numerous things. This might cause echoes, reverberation, or confused sounds, making understanding or communicating in specific contexts difficult.

It is important to moderate your own noise levels, protect your hearing from loud noises, and do your best to stay in spaces that prioritize healthy sounds. Noise reduction methods, adequate sound insulation, and hearing protection in noisy locations can all help offset the potential downsides of sound waves. Remember that while they may cause some problems, the benefits of sound waves and their good effects on your life outweigh any potential drawbacks.

CHAPTER TEN: TELEPHONES

In this chapter, we will explore the world of telephones and how they work. Telephones are incredible, borderline-magical devices that allow us to communicate with people far away. Today it's no big deal for you to call up your friend who moved to Hawaii or message your brother who went off to college, but a few hundred years ago, this would have seemed like complete wizardry!

WHAT IS A TELEPHONE?

A telephone is a device that allows you to communicate with people (or particularly smart pets), whether the two of you are in the same room or thousands of miles away. It comprises various pieces, or *components*, that work together to make it possible. A telephone's basic components are a handset, keypad, and receiver. The handset is the part we hold to our ear and talk into, while the keypad allows us to dial digits to make a call.

Telephones are classified into landline phones, cordless phones, and mobile phones.

Landline phones are conventional telephones that connect calls over physical telephone lines. Cordless phones allow us to walk around the house while conversing within a limited range. Mobile phones, often referred to as *cell phones*, are portable devices that connect calls via wireless networks. Most modern mobile phones provide extra services such as texting, internet access, and apps. Your tablets and smartphones are mobile phones.

HOW SOUND TRAVELS IN A TELEPHONE

Have you ever wondered how voices travel through the telephone when you make a call? When people talk on the telephone, a tiny microphone inside the phone collects the sound waves and turns them into electrical signals. These signals are then transmitted across telephone lines or wireless networks to the person on the other end of the call. The electrical signals are then transformed back into sound waves on the receiver's telephone, and they become audible sounds. It's like a lightning-quick sound trip from your mouth to the other person's ear!

TELEPHONE NUMBERS AND AREA CODES

Every phone has a unique number that allows us to contact the phone's owner; telephone numbers are similar to home addresses. They are made up of a combination of digits you enter through the keypad to contact your friend.

Each telephone number also contains an *area code*. Area codes are used to identify particular areas or countries. For example, a phone number with the area code *212* relates to New York City. Area codes assist in directing calls to the right place and identifying where a call is coming from.

Voicemail

So, what happens when your friend calls, but you are busy and can't answer? In situations like these, *voicemail* and *answering machines* come in handy! They allow callers to leave a message when you can't pick up the phone. Voicemail is a feature provided by telephone service providers that store recorded messages.

Emergency Calls

In an emergency, telephones are essential safety tools. You can call emergency numbers such as 911 in the United States for quick assistance. These numbers connect you to emergency services, including police, fire, and medical aid. It is essential to learn about emergency calls and when to use them. Knowing how to call for help in an emergency can make all the difference!

Telephone Lines and Networks

Telephones are linked through telephone lines. Imagine telephone lines as special channels that transport our voices from one location to another; in fact, they're made up of wires and are often strung alongside power lines. Telephone networks are large grids that connect many places. When you make a phone call, the networks pass your voice down the most direct path to the person you're trying to reach.

Mobile Phones and Wireless Communication

Mobile phones work differently than regular telephones. Mobile phones communicate wirelessly rather than through wires. They use radio waves to convey signals across the air and link to cellular networks. As a result, we can call and send messages from practically everywhere!

Now you understand how telephones work! They are unique devices that allow you to communicate with those far away. Telephones have improved communication, from the fantastic conversion of sound waves into electrical messages to the many telephone networks that guide our voices. So, the next time you pick up the phone, remember the incredible technology that powers it; you may even enjoy chatting with your friends more than normal with this newfound perspective!

CHAPTER ELEVEN: TELEVISION

Television (also called *TV*) is like an enchanted window that gives you glimpses of places far away and times long ago. Although today's TVs are just as colorful and vivid as the world around you, the very first TV sets only showed videos in black and white. Now let's dive in and expand our vision of *television*.

WHAT IS TELEVISION?

Television is a technology that allows you to watch your favorite shows. It has a screen, almost like a window, on which you can watch all kinds of entertaining programs. It also has speakers that play sounds to go along with those programs.

Did you know there are different kinds of televisions? Some have curved screens, while others are flat and very thin. Some televisions can display 3D visuals, giving us a feeling that we are a part of the action! Cool right?

Most modern TV screens use little dots called pixels to create the images you see. Pixels are the millions of tiny bits that come together on some television screens, like tiny jigsaw pieces, to form an image. This means that every image displayed on these televisions is made of tiny pixels. Remote controllers are like magical wands with an invisible connection that allow us to control the TV with the press of a button.

How Images Appear on the Screen

Consider a modern television screen a giant puzzle of pixels, those small, colorful dots we talked about earlier. Each pixel takes on a specific color, forming the images you see when combined. It's similar to creating a mosaic, a picture made up of many individual tiles. That's how your screens' incredible scenes and characters come to life!

Broadcasting Signals

Your favorite shows are sent to your television through special signals. These signals are sent through the air or cables from large towers known as *broadcasting stations*. Broadcasting stations are almost like post offices, delivering messages to your television from afar. These signals represent all the images and sounds needed for your TV to display your favorite shows.

Capturing and Sending Images

Cameras are like the "eyes" of the television. They record everything—sight and sound—and convert it into electrical signals. The cameras used to record television programs are similar to the ones on your phone, except that these cameras send the signals it records from a broadcasting source to your television instead of saving them. That's how scenes from movies, cartoons, and sporting events make their way from the camera to your TV screen.

Sound on Television

Television isn't just about images on a screen; it's also about sound! Along with cameras, microphones, like tiny ears, are used to pick up all voices, music, and sound effects and record them. Microphones convert sounds into electrical signals in the same way that cameras do with images. The signals are then transferred to the television to become sound waves that your brain translates into the sounds you hear.

Remote Control and Buttons

The remote control and TV are connected through more invisible signals. The signal from the remote control is passed through a type of light called *infrared*. The TV receives this signal and reacts to the instructions passed to it. Each button has a special job, like changing channels or turning the TV on and off. It's a cool and convenient way to control your television.

Now you know how television works, from pixels on a screen to broadcasting signals, cameras, microphones, and of course, remote controllers! You've also read several interesting facts about television and its history. The television is an incredible invention that brings joy and excitement to our lives, so grab some popcorn, sit back, and enjoy the wonders of television!

CHAPTER TWELVE: RADIO

Radios are fascinating devices that allow you to listen to music and news and even talk to people who are far away. They're like magic boxes that allow sound to travel rapidly through space. In this chapter, we dive into the curiosities of the radio and how this technology actually works.

WHAT IS A RADIO?

A radio is a device that sends and receives sounds using—you guessed it—radio *waves*. It is a messenger, transporting music, stories, and other auditory information through the air. You can listen to various channels and explore different content on the radio.

HOW RADIO
WAVES TRAVEL

Have you ever wondered how radio waves travel from their sources to your radio? Just like tossing a pebble into a quiet pond and watching the ripples form, radio waves act a lot like water waves. However, they pass through air rather than water.

Radio stations have special equipment that they use to send their broadcasts out in the form of radio waves. Like ripples on the surface of the water, these waves travel in all directions. Each radio station has its frequency, just as everyone has a phone number; when you adjust your radio to a given frequency, the waves are picked up and converted into the audible voices and music coming from the station you have tuned into.

Tuning In to Radio Stations

Radios have a tuning button or dial that allows you to select different radio channels. Each station broadcasts on a unique frequency, which your radio can interpret. Tuning into your favorite station and enjoying its music is as simple as turning the dial or clicking the buttons.

AM and FM Radio

Radio stations broadcast differently, using either AM (Amplitude Modulation) or FM (Frequency Modulation) technology. AM and FM refer to how radio waves are controlled to carry sound.

AM radio is excellent for delivering news, talk shows, and sports commentary. It can travel vast distances and even bounce off the earth's atmosphere, allowing you to listen to distant radio stations.

On the other hand, FM radio is ideal for listening to music. It produces high-quality sound and can send stereo information, making music more lively. However, FM signals do not travel as far, and they can be blocked by hills and even large buildings.

HOW RADIO RECEIVERS WORK

A radio contains different parts that work together to deliver sound to your ears. First, the antenna catches radio waves from the air, collects waves, translates them, and sends them to the receiver. The receiver then extracts specific information, filtering out everything but the station the radio is tuned to. The speaker is the final part, turning electrical signals from the tuner into sound waves. It's like having a tiny band playing inside the radio, creating the music or voices you hear.

Radio Shows and Personalities

Have you ever turned on the radio and heard a voice that made you want to sing along or laugh out loud? That's because radio shows and personalities bring music, stories, and laughter into our homes. Read on to understand the exciting world of radio shows and the amazing people behind them.

Music Shows for Every Taste

Did you know that radio stations offer a wide variety of music shows to keep people listening to their broadcasts? They cater to different musical preferences, from pop hits to rock and roll, country tunes to classical melodies. Tune in to a music show, and you might discover your new favorite song or artist. What's even cooler is that some radio shows even take requests! You can call in and ask the DJ to play your favorite song. It's like having a personal DJ who creates the perfect soundtrack for your day!

Stories That Come Alive

Imagine sitting by the radio, listening to a captivating story unfold as the storyteller perfectly enacts it. Radio shows bring stories to life through the power of sound. You can journey to magical lands, solve mysteries, or embark on thrilling adventures without leaving the comfort of your home.

Radio has brought us countless hours of entertainment, news, and information. From tuning in to your favorite songs to catching up on the latest news, radios connect us to the world around us. The next time you turn on the radio, listen closely to the voices and the stories they tell. Let the music move you, the stories captivate you, and the laughter fills your heart. Embrace the magic of radio shows and personalities and let them be your companions on this incredible audio adventure. Take a moment to appreciate the invisible waves that bring sound to your ears. Who knows? Maybe one day you'll become a radio host, sharing your stories and music with the world.

CHAPTER THIRTEEN:
MICROWAVES

Microwave ovens are electronic devices that use a form of electromagnetic wave called — surprise! — microwaves to heat food speedily. These unique devices have populated just about every home, making it easier to enjoy your favorite meals much more quickly than ever before. In this chapter, you will learn how wonderful and helpful microwaves are and how they work.

WHAT ARE MICROWAVES?

Now, take a moment. You may close your eyes or not; imagine having a super-fast chef who can prepare your favorite meals in minutes. That's exactly what a microwave does! It is a specialized gadget that uses energy to heat and cook food within minutes. Microwaves can interact with many materials to effectively heat or cook food. The waves it produces reflect off the metal interior, pass through materials such as glass, paper, and plastic in the form of heat, and are absorbed by the food, resulting in effective cooking or heating in the kitchen. Microwaves, like radio waves and visible light, are forms of electromagnetic radiation.

HOW MICROWAVES WORK

Microwave ovens operate by producing waves of radiation that stimulate the molecules of whatever liquid or food you place inside. When these molecules get fired up, they begin to move extremely fast, which causes heat to be generated. Microwaves are generated by a mechanism known as a *magnetron*, which acts as the microwave oven's heart.

Microwaves are not only fast but also super convenient. You can heat leftovers, pop popcorn, or even prepare a whole meal using a microwave. The cooking process is simple as can be: place your food in a microwave-safe container, close the door, and set the time and power level. Then, the microwave works its magic, heating your food.

MICROWAVE COMPONENTS

Magnetron: Think of the magnetrons as the heart of the microwave oven. It generates the microwaves that heat the food.

Cavity: The cavity is the internal space where the food is placed for cooking. It is made of metal, which retains and reflects microwaves, directing them toward the food.

Control panel: This is where the power level and other functions, such as the desired cooking time, are found. It may include buttons, knobs, and a digital display.

Turntable: In many microwave ovens, a rotating turntable or tray spins the food while it cooks. This is done to guarantee equal heating.

Door and safety features: To allow you to observe the cooking process, the microwave oven has a door with a window. It also has a door latch and an interlock system that prevents the oven from working while the door is open.

TIPS AND TRICKS

Now that you understand the basics, you should look at some tips and techniques to help you make the most of your microwave.

Proper Containers: Use only microwave-safe containers and lids. Metal containers or plastic containers that are not labeled as microwave-safe should be avoided since they might generate sparks or introduce toxic chemicals into your food.

Stirring and resting: Remember to stir your food occasionally when heating or cooking food in the microwave. This helps distribute the heat evenly. After cooking, give your food some time to cool before eating it. This allows the heat to distribute throughout the food and prevents any burns. Sometimes, you may notice that your food is not heated evenly in the microwave. In cases like this, don't worry too much. Just give it a gentle stir or rotate the dish to help even out the heat distribution.

Microwaving Veggies: Microwaving vegetables is a quick and healthy way to enjoy their goodness. Remember to add a little water and cover the dish to create steam that will help cook the veggies evenly.

Safety First: Always be careful when removing hot food from the microwave. Use oven mitts or pot holders to protect your hands from burns.

Using a microwave requires extra caution, although microwaves do not emit dangerous radiation. Remember how microwaves heat food through radiation, or waves, that produce heat? Radiation can be dangerous for the skin, but microwave radiation is not as dangerous as that of an X-ray machine. Microwave radiation, however, *can* heat up tissues in the body in the same way as it cooks food, and prolonged exposure to microwaves at high levels might result in skin burns or cataracts. So, you must be patient and careful when using the microwave.

While microwaves are a useful cooking tool, they may produce different outcomes than other cooking methods, especially for certain dishes. Some dishes, such as cuts of meat that benefit from browning or crisping, may not reach the desired texture when cooked solely in the microwave. As a result, it is critical to examine the precise cooking requirements of the meal you are going to prepare.

You have just unlocked the secrets of the amazing microwave oven. From heating up snacks to preparing delicious meals in a flash, microwaves have changed how food is cooked and eaten. So, the next time you use this magical appliance, remember the science behind it and enjoy the convenience it brings to your kitchen.

CHAPTER FOURTEEN: COMPUTERS

Now we'll dive into yet another fascinating tool of the modern world: computers. With these machines essentially everywhere you look, there's little doubt you've wondered at some point, "How do these actually work?"

Well, you curious cats are in luck! In this chapter, we will walk you through the fascinating world of computers and explore how they operate, what they can do, and some mind-blowing facts about them.

WHAT IS A COMPUTER?

Let's start with the basics. A computer is a device powered by electricity, just like a television; it can *process*, *store*, and *retrieve* information. These are just fancy ways of saying that a computer *works* with certain things, *saves* certain things, and also *gets* certain things. But a computer is not simply an ordinary worker shuffling information back and forth. Today's computers can perform basic functions *10 million times faster* than the human brain. Computers exist in various sizes and designs, including desktop, laptop, tablet, and smartphone models. Whatever the type of computer is, it must have a screen, a keyboard/keypad, and a mouse or other way to interact with it.

Every computer is made up of several components. You can think of them as the memory, brain, and input (your keyboard or mouse) and output (including your screen and speaker) devices. Computers use their *central processing unit* (CPU) to do calculations and make decisions in much the same way as our brains process information.

HOW COMPUTERS COMMUNICATE

Humans communicate by speaking to each other using audible languages, but did you know that computers use languages, too? Computers use something called *software,* a set of instructions that tells a computer what to do. Computer software is developed or created using programming languages. These programming languages have specific rules, just like the languages humans use to communicate.

Once the software is created, it acts like a recipe for a cake. Do you know how a recipe tells you what ingredients to use and how to put them together to make a cake? Each different type of software tells the computer what instructions to follow to do something, like play a game, make a sketch, or write a story.

INSIDE A COMPUTER

It's time to look inside a computer to learn more about what happens there. Different parts of computers work together to carry out tasks. Something called *random-access memory* (RAM) enables the computer to do and save numerous tasks simultaneously, and the hard drive saves data. The RAM acts as the computer's short-term memory, while the hard drive is its long-term memory.

The motherboard connects all the computer's components using circuits, which act a lot like your body's circulatory system. Within these circuits are small electrical switches called *transistors*, which are used in computers as tiny on/off switches.

WHAT COMPUTERS CAN DO

Computers are capable of so many amazing things! They open up a whole world of exciting new capabilities and opportunities for everybody. You can use computers to explore educational websites and programs, learn new things, and work on projects with friends.

Thanks to the enjoyable and interactive learning environments computers create, you can better understand complex ideas through exciting multimedia. Computers are like magical devices that can make ideas come to life. They allow us to travel the globe, interact with others, and create incredible things.

Using Computers

Computers have become integral to a lot of young people's lives globally, offering numerous benefits and opportunities. Some of them are:

Learning and Education: Computers offer the opportunity to access many educational resources, interactive learning programs, and online courses. You can read up on various subjects, practice skills, engage in virtual experiments, and gain knowledge just like you do in a classroom. You can learn new languages and even meet speakers of that language; all of these are possible with your computer.

Creativity and Artistic Expression: Computers open up a world of creativity for you! You can learn to edit videos and images and produce digital art and music. You can use graphic design software to sketch and paint, bringing your imagination to life.

Communication and Collaboration: You can communicate with friends worldwide through computers. You can contact your loved ones via video calls, instant messaging, and social media platforms. Computers also make it easier for you to collaborate on group projects, share ideas, and learn from one another.

Organization and productivity: You can use computers to keep organized and complete tasks better. It's easier to stay on top of your assignments and duties using productivity tools like calendars, to-do lists, and note-taking applications. Additionally, computers make it simpler to do research, gather data, and present your research for school projects.

CHAPTER FIFTEEN:
THE INTERNET

The Internet is an incredible network that connects people and their computers all around the world. You've wondered how computers work, but have you ever wondered how the network that connects computers to each other works? Whether you have or haven't, in this chapter, you're sure to learn a lot as we dive into the world of the Internet and how it connects *billions* of people across the planet. Get ready to embark on a digital adventure as we explore the fascinating world of the Internet!

WHAT IS THE INTERNET?

The Internet is a global computer network that allows you to communicate, share information, and access various services online. Millions of computers, smartphones, and other devices worldwide are connected by it like a huge web. Think of it as a huge library where you can access information, play games, watch films, and connect with your friends.

HOW THE INTERNET WORKS

Internet Service Providers (ISPs): Internet service providers are like the bridge connecting your device to the Internet. They provide you access to the internet through cables, satellite, or wireless technologies. Think of an ISP as a portal that connects you to the digital world.

Data Packets: Information is divided into smaller units known as *data packets* when sent or received over the Internet. These packets pass through switches and routers, which act as traffic controllers to ensure they reach their destination quickly.

IP addresses: Remember how each telephone has a number, and each house has an address? Each Internet-connected device has a special identification number known as an *Internet Protocol*, or *IP*, *address*. Information can be sent to the appropriate device using this form of a digital address.

World Wide Web: Through web browsers like Chrome, Firefox, or Safari, you may access the *World Wide Web,* sometimes known as simply "the Web," a collection of websites and web pages. It resembles a virtual treasure chest that houses information, entertainment, and interaction opportunities.

Exploring the Internet: Searching and browsing the web using a search engine is often referred to as "exploring" the Internet. A search engine is like a magnifying glass that hovers over a lot of information and picks out what you need, then zooms in on it for you to see. One popular search engine is Google. Have you ever used a search engine? You can look for trivia, school assistance, or a recipe for your favorite dish. Browsing allows you to visit websites, read articles, watch videos, and explore different online platforms.

USING THE INTERNET

Let's take a look at all the awesome ways you can make the most of the Internet:

Education and Learning: Did you know that specific websites and games on the Internet are designed to help you learn new things? You can find entertaining movies, engaging tests, and interesting events to aid your studies in math, science, history, and other subjects. It's like having a clever friend who enjoys passing along exciting information!

Online Libraries: Does your school library close after school hours? Having access to the Internet is like having a library that is always open. Amazing digital libraries containing many books, stories, and articles are available online and ready to read. You can go on excursions, encounter fascinating people, and learn about various subjects online without ever leaving home!

Hobbies and Creativity: Are you prepared to apply all of your super-creative abilities? The Internet can be of assistance! You'll find fantastic tutorials and movies that teach you how to code, craft, paint, and draw. It's like having a digital art studio where you can produce incredible works of art and show them to your friends!

Fun and Entertainment: Who says using the Internet can't be fun? There are so many fun activities available online! You can watch amusing films and cartoons that make you laugh aloud, play challenging games that push your brain, and even listen to upbeat music that makes you want to dance around the room. It's like throwing yourself an endless party!

CHAPTER SIXTEEN:
SMARTPHONES

Here's another technology you encounter every day! You already know what a smartphone is, but do you know how it works or how it's made? Let's dive in and discover the wonders of these remarkable devices!

WHAT IS A SMARTPHONE?

Imagine having a device that can do almost anything you can think of, a device that has limitless capabilities; that device is a smartphone! A smartphone is a minicomputer, camera, music player, and many more devices in a small, portable box. It serves as your digital assistant, source of entertainment, and link to the online world.

USING A SMARTPHONE

Using a smartphone, you can communicate instantly with your friends and family. You can call, text, or even use video chat to interact. It's like having a magical gateway that reduces distances and connects family members and friends.

Software Applications: Smartphones have access to a universe of applications, or apps, created by people for your use. You can download and use them for various purposes. Want to play games, learn a new language, or chat with your friends? These days, there's an app for everything!

The Internet: A smartphone can provide access to the Internet. You may browse web pages, watch movies, and search for facts and the history of any subject you can think of. It's like carrying a portable digital encyclopedia that can answer your questions.

Making and Keeping Memories: Smartphones are equipped with cameras that allow you to capture moments quickly. Save the memories of your experiences by taking pictures and recording videos. Your smartphone is your dependable partner in making priceless reminders of good memories.

Entertainment in your pocket: Your smartphone has everything you need for enjoyment and relaxation when the time comes. Watch funny videos, stream movies, and listen to your favorite music. It's like always having a mobile entertainment center with you.

SMARTPHONE PARTS

Let's take a closer look at the different parts that make up a smartphone:

Display: The screen you see on the front of your smartphone is called the *display*. That's where you see all the data, pictures, and movies. It is a window into digital technology, where you may use apps and discover the material.

Buttons: Numerous smartphone buttons allow you to browse and manage the device; most often used are the power, volume, and home buttons. You can use these buttons to control the volume, turn your smartphone on and off, and return to the home screen.

Camera: Cameras are an essential part of smartphones. You can use it to record precious moments and memories through images and videos. To improve your shooting experience, some smartphones even contain numerous cameras with various features, such as wide-angle or telephoto lenses.

Microphone and speaker: You can hear audio and communicate with people thanks to these parts. The microphone enables you to talk and be heard during phone calls or voice recordings, while the speaker allows you to listen to music, watch videos, and hear phone calls.

Processor: Your smartphone's processor is its brain. Thanks to the strong chips handling all calculations and operations, your programs will function smoothly and swiftly. It controls how quickly and effectively your device operates.

Battery: A battery powers your smartphone. It supplies the power required to keep your device functioning all day by storing electrical energy. You can keep using your smartphone by charging it to refuel the battery.

Storage: The built-in storage that comes with smartphones allows you to store items like images, videos, and apps. It functions as a digital safe for all of your data. A memory card can be used to increase the capacity of some cell phones.

Connectivity: Smartphones are made to keep you in touch with the outside world. They have a range of connectivity choices, including cellular networks, Wi-Fi, and Bluetooth. These enable wireless internet access, file sharing, and interpersonal communication.

When you use your smartphone...

Remember that balance is key. Enjoy your smartphone, but remember to find a healthy balance between screen time and other activities. Make time for reading, outdoor adventures and exercise, and face-to-face interactions with friends and family. Stay safe while using your smartphone online. Be cautious about sharing personal information and only interact with people you know and trust. If in doubt, always seek guidance from a trusted adult.

CHAPTER SEVENTEEN: CAMERAS

WHAT IS
A CAMERA?

A camera is a device that helps you capture and save moments as pictures or videos. Although today cameras are almost synonymous with smartphones, cameras are available in different shapes and sizes. Some are quite big, while others are small enough to fit in a pocket or your smartphone. However, no matter how the cameras look, they all work similarly.

When you take a picture using a digital camera, the image is recorded on a memory card inside the camera. However, if you use an older film camera, the image is preserved on a particular piece of thin plastic called *film*. You must then take the film to a photo studio to process it and get your pictures, which are called *photographs*. Many digital cameras also have screens on the back that allow you to see the picture you take immediately. That way, you can ensure you captured the moment just as you wanted.

Cameras are amazing because they allow you to capture special memories, like birthdays, vacations, or even just everyday moments with friends and family. You can look back at the pictures and videos you take and remember all the fun times you had. A camera comprises several parts that work together to capture and create photographs.

THE MAIN PARTS
OF A CAMERA

The lens: The lens functions as the camera's eye. It is a piece of transparent glass or plastic that permits light to enter the camera. The lens directs light onto the image sensor, helping you take a sharp, clear image. Different lenses have different features, such as zooming in or capturing a wider picture.

The image sensor: The image sensor functions as the camera's brain. A specific component within the camera collects light and turns it into an electrical signal. The image sensor in the latest cameras allows you to capture digital images.

The shutter: The shutter is like a door or a curtain in front of the image sensor. It controls the time the image sensor is exposed to light. When you click the button to take a picture, the shutter opens, allowing light to reach the image sensor. After a brief moment, the shutter closes, ending the exposure and capturing the image.

The viewfinder: The viewfinder on a camera is a little window through which you can see the environment you want to capture. It assists you in framing your shot and deciding what to include in the image. Some cameras utilize an optical viewfinder using mirrors, while others use an electronic viewfinder with a tiny screen.

The camera body and controls: The body is the outer covering that houses all the camera's internal components. The different buttons and controls on the camera body allow you to customize settings such as focus, exposure, and flash. These options allow you to modify your images and make them look precisely how you want them to.

CARING FOR
YOUR CAMERA

Keep it clean: Regularly clean your camera's body and lens to eliminate dust, dirt, and fingerprints. Use a soft, lint-free cloth or a camera cleaning kit designed exclusively for cameras. Avoid using harsh or abrasive chemicals that could scratch the lens or camera body.

Use a camera bag: Keep your camera in a bag or case when you aren't using it. This will shield it from bumps, scratches, and dust. Choose a bag with adequate padding and separate compartments to keep your camera and accessories safe and organized.

Protect it from extreme conditions: Avoid exposing your camera to high humidity, harsh temperatures, or excessive moisture. Extreme temperatures can harm internal components and impair camera operation. Use a moisture-absorbing package or a dry cabinet to safeguard your camera in a humid environment.

Handle with care: Always use clean hands to operate your camera's settings, buttons, and lenses, and be careful when taking pictures. Avoid touching the image sensor or the mirror as much as possible. Change lenses in a clean and dust-free environment to avoid particles getting inside the camera.

Use lens caps and filters: Lens caps should be used to cover your lenses when not in use to prevent scratches and dust buildup. Consider using protective filters to protect your lens from possible harm. Filters are easier to replace and less expensive than fixing or replacing a lens.

Be cautious with batteries: Charge and store camera batteries according to the manufacturer's recommendations. Avoid overcharging or completely discharging the batteries by using the proper charger. Remove the batteries from your camera if you will not use them for an extended period to prevent corrosion.

Regular maintenance: Regularly check the user's manual for recommended maintenance procedures. Some cameras may require sensor cleaning or software updates, which should be performed by a professional or according to the manufacturer's recommendations.

CHAPTER EIGHTEEN: REMOTE CONTROLS

A *remote control* is a small device that lets you control other electronic devices from a distance without needing to physically touch them. When you press a button, the remote control sends a command, and the device paired with it, such as a TV, receives the message. Imagine sitting on the couch watching your favorite TV show and wanting to change the channel or adjust the volume; you can use a remote control instead of going to the TV.

HOW REMOTE CONTROLS WORK

A remote control uses special light called *infrared* to send signals to the device you want to control. These signals are like secret codes that tell the device what to do. When you press a button on the remote control, it sends out a signal by flashing light, which then travels through the air to the receiving device. Take the TV as an example. When you press the button to change the channel, the remote control sends a signal to the TV that says, "Hey, I want to switch to a different channel!" The TV receives the signal, understands the command, and changes to your selected channel.

A remote control can be used to control various devices, not just TVs. You can use them to control DVD players, video game consoles, audio systems, air conditioners, and toys. Each device has its own specific remote control that works with it. Each remote control has specific buttons for different functions. For example, you may have buttons to turn the device on or off, adjust the volume, change channels, pause or play a movie, and navigate menus. Some remote controls also have special buttons, like a "mute" button to turn off the sound temporarily or a "menu" button to access settings.

One important thing to remember is that remote controls use batteries to work. It's a good idea to keep extra batteries handy and replace old ones when they run out of power. Remote controls make managing electronic devices from a distance easy and convenient, like little helpers that save you from getting up and allow you to have more control over your devices without even touching them.

ADVANTAGES OF REMOTE CONTROLS

Convenience: The main advantage of a remote control is convenience. It allows you to control electronic devices from a distance without needing to touch or be close to them physically. This means you can operate devices like TVs, DVD players, or audio systems from the comfort of your couch or bed.

Ease of use: Remote controls are generally designed to be user-friendly, with clearly labeled buttons and intuitive layouts. They are designed to make it easy for anyone to control devices without complicated instructions or technical knowledge.

Accessibility: Remote controls can be particularly helpful for individuals with mobility issues or physical limitations. They provide an accessible way to operate devices without needing to move around or exert physical effort.

Efficiency: With a remote control, you can quickly and efficiently navigate menus, change settings, or switch between channels or inputs. It takes less time and effort compared to manually operating the device's controls or buttons.

Multiple device control: Many remote controls can be programmed to work with multiple devices. This means you can use a single remote to control your TV, DVD player, and sound system, eliminating the need for separate remotes for each device.

DISADVANTAGES

Loss or misplacement: Remote controls are small and can be easily misplaced or lost. When this happens, it can be frustrating because you may not be able to control your devices until the remote is found or replaced.

Battery dependency: Remote controls require batteries to function, and when the batteries run out, the remote won't work until they are replaced. This means you need to keep spare batteries handy and remember to change them when needed.

Line of sight requirement: Many remote controls operate using infrared (IR) signals, which require a direct line of sight between the remote and the device being controlled. If there are obstacles or if you are in a different room, the signal may not reach the device, making the remote ineffective.

Compatibility limitations: Not all devices are compatible with universal remote controls, and some devices require specific remote models. You may need multiple remotes for different devices, leading to clutter and confusion.

Complexity for some users: While remote controls are designed to be user-friendly, it's only inevitable that someone gets a little confused once and a while (and sometimes the manual can seem to be of little help!). The multiple buttons and functions can be overwhelming for those who need to become more familiar with the technology.

It is important to note that the advantages and disadvantages of remote controls can vary depending on the specific device and user preferences.

In conclusion, remote controls have changed how people interact with their electronic devices. Their convenience and versatility have made them an essential tool in homes and offices. From controlling televisions and audio systems to smart home devices, the remote control has simplified people's lives, offering an effortless user experience.

CHAPTER NINETEEN:
VEHICLES

A *vehicle* is a machine that helps you move from one place to another. It's a special tool of transportation that takes you away on journeys. There are many types of vehicles, and each of them is designed for a slightly different purpose or reason.

Let's take a look at some of the most common kinds of vehicles:

Cars: Cars, also known as *automobiles*, are four-wheeled vehicles primarily designed for personal transportation. They come in various sizes, from compact cars to sedans, to luxury cars like limousines. Cars are widely used for commuting, family transportation, and personal travel.

Trucks: Trucks are larger vehicles designed for transporting goods or heavy loads. They vary in size, from pickup trucks to commercial trucks, such as delivery trucks, box trucks, and tractor-trailers. Trucks are commonly used in the transportation, construction, and logistics industries.

Motorcycles: Motorcycles are two-wheeled vehicles powered by an engine. They are popular for their agility, speed, and fuel efficiency. Motorcycles can be further categorized into types such as sport bikes, cruisers, touring bikes, and off-road bikes. They are commonly used for personal commuting, recreational riding, and racing.

Bicycles: Bicycles are human-powered vehicles with two wheels. They are a popular means of transportation, exercise, and recreation. Bicycles come in various forms, including road, mountain, hybrid, and city bikes. They are environmentally friendly and promote physical fitness.

Buses: Buses are large vehicles designed to carry multiple passengers. They come in different sizes, such as city buses, coach buses, school buses, and shuttle buses. Buses are commonly used for public transit systems, school transportation, and group travel.

Vans: Vans are vehicles designed for transporting passengers or cargo. They provide more space and seating capacity than cars. Vans come in various configurations, including passenger, cargo, minivans, and camper vans. They are commonly used for family travel, commercial cargo, and recreational camping.

SUVs (Sport Utility Vehicles): SUVs are versatile vehicles that combine elements of cars and trucks. They offer a higher seating position, ample cargo space, and the ability to handle off-road conditions. SUVs come in different sizes, from compact to full-size, and are popular for their versatility and ruggedness.

Recreational Vehicles (RVs): RVs combine living accommodations with transportation. They are often used for long-distance travel, camping, and road trips. RVs include motorhomes, camper vans, travel trailers, and fifth-wheel trailers.

These are just a few examples of the many types of vehicles available. Each type serves a unique purpose, catering to diverse transportation needs and requirements. There are many different types of vehicles, but the focus in this chapter is on cars since they are the most common type people use daily.

THE CAR
AS A VEHICLE

A car is a four-wheeled vehicle with seats for people and trunk space for carrying things. It has an engine, which acts like the car's heart and uses fuel, such as gasoline or electricity, to make it move. When you want to travel or go somewhere, you get into the car, buckle your seat belts, and the engine powers the car to move forward.

Cars have different parts that work together to make them move and keep you safe. Here are some important parts of a car:

Wheels: Cars have four wheels that help them roll on the ground. Wheels have tires made of rubber that provide a smooth ride and grip the road so the car doesn't slip.

Steering Wheel: The steering wheel is in front of the driver's seat. It allows the driver to control the direction of the car. When the driver turns the steering wheel, the car turns left or right.

Engine: The engine is the part of the car that makes it move. It burns fuel or uses electricity to create power. The engine is usually located in the front of the car, under the hood.

Brakes: Brakes are the parts of the car that help it slow down and stop. When the driver presses the brake pedal, it applies pressure to the wheels, causing them to stop spinning.

Seat Belts: Seat belts are important safety devices in cars. They are straps that cross your body and keep you secure in your seat. Seat belts help protect you in case of a sudden stop or accident.

Lights: Cars have headlights in the front that illuminate the road at night and make the car visible to others. They also have tail lights at the back that signal when the car brakes or turns.

It is important to remember that driving a car is a big responsibility and requires a driver's license and adult supervision. It is crucial to follow traffic rules, pay attention to the road, and prioritize safety. To summarize, a vehicle, like a car, is a machine with wheels and other important parts that help you move from one place to another. It is a fantastic way to explore the world and make unforgettable memories with family and friends.

In conclusion, vehicles are incredible machines that help you move from one place to another. Each vehicle has unique features and purposes, whether cars, bikes, trains, or rockets. They make your life more convenient, allow you to explore, and connect you with people and places.

CHAPTER TWENTY: ENGINES

An engine is like the heart of a machine; engines power many things you use daily, such as cars, motorcycles, and even some toys. Think of an engine as a special device that can turn fuel, like gasoline or electricity, into motion or movement. It is a truly marvelous piece of technology, and just like you need food to have energy, an engine needs fuel to create the power it produces.

IMPORTANT PARTS
OF AN ENGINE

Cylinder: An engine has one or more *cylinders*. A cylinder is a tube where fuel and air mix together and combust or burn, creating power.

Piston: Inside each cylinder, there is a part called a *piston*. A piston is a small, round metal block that moves up and down. When the fuel and air combust, they push the piston down, creating force.

Crankshaft: The force from the piston is then transferred to a part called the *crankshaft*. The crankshaft is a long, spinning rod. It takes the piston's up-and-down motion and turns it into a circular motion, like a spinning wheel.

Spark Plug: The engine uses a spark plug to make the fuel and air burn inside the cylinder. The spark plug creates a tiny spark that ignites the fuel mixture, just like a tiny lightning bolt.

Exhaust: After the fuel and air combust, they become hot gasses. These gasses need to escape from the engine, so there is a special path called the *exhaust* system. It guides the gasses out of the engine, allowing fresh fuel and air to come in.

COMMON USES
OF ENGINES

Transportation: Engines power motor vehicles, including cars, trucks, motorcycles, trains, ships, airplanes, and spacecraft. Internal combustion engines and jet engines are among the propulsion systems used to propel these vehicles.

Industrial machinery: Engines are used in various industrial settings to power machinery and equipment. This includes generators, pumps, compressors, construction equipment (excavators and bulldozers), agricultural machinery (tractors and harvesters), manufacturing machinery, and mining equipment.

Power generation: Engines work in some power plants to generate electricity. Steam turbines, gas turbines, and internal combustion engines (such as diesel and gas engines) drive electrical generators to produce power. The engines in power plants may use fossil fuels, natural gas, or biomass.

Marine propulsion: Engines power boats, ships, and submarines, enabling marine transportation and exploration. Marine engines include diesel engines, gas turbines, and steam engines, depending on the vessel's size and purpose.

Aerospace and space exploration: Rocket engines propel spacecraft, satellites, and rockets into space. These powerful engines are designed to operate in the vacuum of space and provide the necessary thrust to overcome Earth's gravity and achieve orbital or interplanetary trajectories.

Emergency power backup: Engines, particularly generators, are used as backup power sources during emergencies or in areas with unreliable or limited electrical grid access. These backup systems ensure a continuous power supply in critical situations such as hospitals, data centers, and residential homes.

Recreational vehicles: Engines power recreational vehicles (RVs), including motorhomes and camper vans, providing mobility and onboard amenities such as lighting, heating, and cooling systems.

Lawn and garden equipment: Small engines can be used to power a variety of lawn care and gardening equipment, such as lawnmowers, chainsaws, leaf blowers, and garden tractors.

Aircraft and aviation: Engines, including jet engines, turboprop engines, and piston engines, are used for commercial and private aviation, military aircraft, and unmanned aerial vehicles (drones).

Stationary engines: Engines can be used as stationary power sources in various applications, such as industrial facilities, agricultural operations, remote power stations, and construction sites.

These are just a few examples of the numerous applications and uses of engines across various industries. Engines provide the necessary power and propulsion for various vehicles, machinery, and systems, enabling human mobility, industrial operations, and technological advancements.

Engines are incredibly clever because they can make thousands of these explosions happen every minute. The more explosions they make, the more power they create. Different types of engines work in different ways, but no matter the type, engines are about turning fuel into power and making things move. It is important to remember that engines are powerful and can be dangerous if not used properly. That's why only grown-ups who know how to operate them should handle engines in vehicles or machinery.

To wrap up, engines are like the hearts of machines, turning fuel into power and making things move. They are the secret behind cars, planes, and even rockets. Understanding how engines work opens up a world of possibilities and sparks curiosity about the wonders of technology. Remember, engines are powerful and should be handled with care.

CHAPTER TWENTY-ONE: ROCKETS

A rocket is the champion of all machines; it is an outlier, even among very complex and powerful technology. A rocket has a long, slender body with a pointed end called the *nose cone*. Inside the rocket is a powerful engine that burns special fuel to create a tremendous amount of *thrust* or push. The fuel mixture consists of chemicals that, when ignited, produce a controlled explosion. This explosion creates a force that pushes the rocket upward with incredible speed.

At the rocket's base is a part called the *nozzle*. The nozzle helps direct the burning fuel's hot gasses, creating a powerful jet of gas that shoots out from the back of the rocket. This force, known as thrust, pushes the rocket forward and propels it into the sky. Rockets need an incredible amount of power to reach outer space because they have to overcome Earth's gravity, which tries to pull everything down. Once the rocket is high enough, it can escape the pull of gravity and travel through space.

Rockets are complex vehicles used for space exploration, satellite launches, and other applications. They have several key components that work together to achieve propulsion and control. Here are the main components of a rocket:

Payload: The *payload* refers to the cargo or equipment the rocket carries. It could be a satellite, scientific instrument, crewed spacecraft, or other payload specific to the mission objectives.

Rocket engine: The rocket engine generates thrust by expelling high-speed exhaust gasses. It is the primary component that propels the rocket. Rocket engines can be liquid-fueled or solid-fueled, depending on the design.

Propellant tanks: Rockets require *propellants, or fuel,* for combustion in the rocket engine. Propellant tanks store liquid or solid fuels, such as liquid oxygen (LOX), liquid hydrogen (LH2), kerosene, or solid rocket fuel. These tanks are usually pressurized to ensure a constant flow of fuel to the engine.

Thrust structure: The *thrust structure* supports and connects the rocket engine to the rest of the rocket structure. It withstands the powerful thrust generated during engine ignition and helps transfer this force to the rocket's body.

Guidance system: Rockets are equipped with *guidance systems* to control their trajectory and orientation during flight. These systems may include things like gyroscopes, accelerometers, sensors, and computers to collect data, make calculations, and adjust the rocket's path accordingly.

Avionics: *Avionics* refers to the electronic systems on board the rocket. These include communication, telemetry, navigation, and control systems. Avionics is crucial in monitoring and controlling various aspects of the rocket's flight.

Structural components: The rocket's structure comprises various components that provide strength and support. These include the main body or *airframe, interstage sections* to connect different parts of the rocket, *fairings* (protective coverings for the payload), and fins for stabilization and control.

Stage separation systems: Rockets often have multiple *stages* containing engines and fuel. Stage separation systems facilitate the separation of used stages to reduce weight and allow subsequent stages to continue the ascent. These systems may include separation motors, explosive bolts, or other mechanisms.

Thermal protection systems: Rockets that experience extreme temperatures during launch and re-entry may incorporate thermal protection systems. These systems help protect the rocket and its payload from the intense heat generated during atmospheric re-entry or exposure to the space environment.

Each component of a rocket plays a crucial role in achieving successful launch, flight, and mission objectives. The design and configuration of these components may vary depending on the specific rocket type, mission requirements, and desired performance.

Rockets are used for many important things, such as

Space exploration: Rockets are used to launch spacecraft, like satellites, telescopes, and even manned missions to explore other planets. They help scientists learn more about space, study distant stars and galaxies, and understand our universe better.

Satellite deployment: Satellites launched by rockets orbit the Earth and provide important services, like TV and radio signals, internet connectivity, and GPS navigation. They also perform various tasks like weather monitoring and environmental observations. Rockets play a crucial role in maintaining these communication networks.

Scientific research: Rockets carry scientific experiments into space, allowing scientists to study the effects of space travel on the human body, conduct experiments in microgravity, and learn more about the Earth's atmosphere.

Space Station resupply: Rockets send supplies, food, and equipment to astronauts living on space stations like the International Space Station (ISS). They ensure that astronauts have what they need to live and work in space.

Rockets are amazing machines that open humans up to the wonders of space exploration. They require careful engineering, precise calculations, and dedicated teams of scientists and engineers to make them work. They have helped humanity as a whole to discover new things about the vast universe we live in and who we are as inhabitants of not only planet Earth but the entire universe around us.

CHAPTER TWENTY-TWO: AIRPLANES

WHAT IS AN AIRPLANE?

Have you ever boarded a plane and could not help but wonder how something as *huge* as that could carry so many people and yet still glide seamlessly through the sky? Sit tight as you are about to be wowed by what this thing is and how it does what it does best: fly!

An airplane (often shortened to "plane") is a giant vehicle shaped like a bird and built to fly in the sky. Like a bird, it has two wings that keep the air underneath them suppressed while the airplane lifts itself up and an engine that helps it stay working as it runs, flies, and lands without difficulty.

Some of the most important parts of every airplane are:

Wings: An airplane's wings are usually positioned on each side. They function to help it take lift and suspend itself in the sky. They have moving parts called *flaps* and *slats*, which are like little doors on the wings that the pilot can open and close. When they are opened, the wings become bigger and more powerful and help the plane fly faster and land smoothly.

Engine: The engine, just as in other vehicles, powers the plane to start working before helping it propel itself on the runway before it takes off. The two main types of airplane engines are *reciprocating engines* and *jet engines*. Reciprocating engines are mostly used in small planes, and they work like the engines in cars; they have pistons that go up and down, and the movement turns the propeller. The propeller is basically a big fan that blows the air backward with great force, making the plane move forward. Jet engines help the plane move in a different way. They have a large fan that absorbs air instead of pushing it backward; the air is then mixed with fuel, which causes an ignition. The explosion from the ignition produces hot exhaust gasses that shoot from the back of

94

the engine. The force of the exhaust escaping helps the plane to move forward.

Landing gear: The *landing gear* helps the plane take off to the sky and land safely when it gets to its destination. It comprises four wheels altogether – two in front of the plane and two at the rear, with shock-absorbing devices that cushion the plane as it touches the ground and helps to stabilize its movement. Some planes have wheels that can fold into the plane after takeoff, while others just leave their wheels hanging outside as they fly.

Body: The plane's *body* consists of the section where passengers sit, the cargo, and the *cockpit*, where the pilots control the flight from.

HOW AIRPLANES FLY

Now that you understand some of the parts of the airplane and what they do, here's a cool way to understand how they all combine to help the plane lift itself and go straight to the sky. To achieve this, four main forces act on the plane: *thrust, drag, lift,* and *gravity.*

Thrust: This force pushes the plan forward before it lifts itself. It is caused by the working of the parts inside the engines or propellers that you have just learned about.

Drag: This is the force that slows down the plane as it flies. It is caused by resistance in the air as the plane glides through it.

Lift: This force helps the plane to remain in the air for as long as it needs to. It is caused by the shape of the plane's wing while in the air. When the wings are curved at the top and flat at the base, the shape causes air to flow faster over the top than the base. When the air flows faster at the top than at the base, the air pressure is also different; it is usually lower at the top and higher at the base. This difference in pressure then keeps the wing up and helps it to achieve lift.

Gravity: Gravity is the force that pulls everything down toward the ground. Thrust and lift act against gravity to help the plane take off and stay in the air. When the plane is landing, however, the pilot raises the flaps and slats on the wings in order to reduce lift. The lower the lift force, the slower the plane gets and then lands safely.

FUN FACTS ABOUT AIRPLANES

- The first people to fly a plane in the air were the Wright Brothers, who achieved this success on December 17, 1903.
- The record for the world's longest continuous flight was set in 1959 by Robert Timm and his co-pilot John Cook. They flew for 64 days, 22 hours, and 19 minutes.
- The fastest airplane ever built was the Lockheed SR-71 Blackbird, reaching more than 3,500 kph.

CHAPTER TWENTY-THREE: HELICOPTERS

Like an airplane, a helicopter (often called a "chopper") is a vehicle designed to fly through the skies. Although helicopters and airplanes both soar through the air, there are some crucial differences between the two of them. Hop aboard as we hover on over to some of the coolest helicopter facts.

WHAT MAKES HELICOPTERS SPECIAL?

Unlike airplanes, which must move forward, gaining speed to take off, helicopters can be flown directly up, left, right, and even backward! Not only that, but helicopters can hover, stay put in the air, and even fly around a single spot; that's why you often find one in a scene where it's difficult to rescue people or where people are lost in tight places. The unique ability of a helicopter makes it a go-to vehicle when it comes to search and rescue operations because of its ability to fly very close to the ground and land on smaller and rougher surfaces like rooftops, grass, hilltops, and roads, unlike airplanes.

IMPORTANT PARTS OF HELICOPTERS

Main rotor: A helicopter's main *rotor* is the blades on top that help it take flight. It is a central part of the body of any helicopter. It works by spinning rapidly to help the helicopter gather enough force to lift itself. It is made of several long blades connected to a central hub, which is in turn connected to the helicopter's roof by a *rotor mast,* which is a metal rod that holds the main rotor up.

Pitch Control: The pilot can control how the main rotor works from the cockpit using either the *collective pitch control* or the *cyclic pitch control.* The collective pitch control is used to control the main rotor's speed, while the cyclic pitch control is like a stick used to direct the helicopter left, right, up, or down. These directions are best known to pilots as *pitch* (up and down movement), *roll* (left to right or side to side movement), and *yaw* (the helicopter's forward or backward movement).

Engine: A helicopter's engine is located inside its body, not visible except when the body is opened up. Once it's in operation, it generates power through pistons, which we learned about in Chapter 23; their movement helps convert fuel into mechanical energy. This energy then turns a shaft, which ends up turning the main rotor.

Cockpit: A helicopter's cockpit, where the pilots sit, is always at the front. It is the section of the helicopter where every functioning part is controlled from. It contains two seats for the pilots, the instrument panel that displays how well the instruments are performing, the tail rotor pedals, the collective pitch control, and the cyclic pitch control.

Landing gear: A helicopter's landing gear is the part that comes in contact with the ground. Most helicopters' landing gear has either two wheels, two *skids*—which look a bit like skis—or even *floats*, which allow safe landing on water. The type of landing gear a helicopter is equipped with depends on its size and what it's used for, but all landing gear's main purpose is to help it stabilize when not in flight mode. The landing gear is crucial, as it helps prevent the helicopter from losing balance when it takes off or lands and avoids any damage when it lands on rough surfaces.

HOW HELICOPTERS FLY

Just like a plane, a helicopter flies using its own form of wings, except that its wings are not static to its sides; they are long, thin blades that spin whenever it is about to take flight or is in the air. The blades and every other part connected to them (altogether called the main rotor) are all linked directly to the helicopter's engine. Once the engine is started, it forces the main rotor to spin the blades.

Just as air pressure acting against an airplane's wings controls its lift and speed, air also pushes against a helicopter's blades and creates air pressure. The pilot controls how the blades spin (also affecting how the air hits them in the process) and how much force the engine puts on the main rotor. This controls a helicopter's direction and speed while flying.

While the main rotor keeps working at the top of the helicopter, a smaller rotor at the tail regulates how stable the helicopter stays during flight. It prevents the helicopter from spinning randomly and losing direction.

While a helicopter ride can be fun, it may not be the safest option for kids. Even though the blades are far above, they still gather a huge amount of force, and the wind they generate can blow away lightweight objects or kids who come close to them during takeoff. Now that you understand the major differences between an airplane and a helicopter, you can take a guess at what mission a helicopter is on when one cruises over your rooftop!

CHAPTER TWENTY-FOUR: BOATS

Ever been on a cruise before? Maybe you've gazed out the window at the ocean beneath you and wondered how it was possible for such a massive object to glide across the water. Is there something underwater that pushes the boat and makes it stay on the surface of the water? Is there some sort of strange voodoo magic or wizardry at play? Well, grab your life jackets and prepare to dive (safely!) overboard as we investigate just what it is that allows ships to glide across the water's surface.

WHAT IS
A BOAT?

Just like airplanes and helicopters are *aircraft* because they operate in the air, boats are *watercraft* because they float on the water. A boat is a type of vehicle specialized to transport people on the water. A boat is not as large a ship; in fact, it can fit into a ship conveniently. It can also be easily carried out of the water and back because of its small size. It's one of the most popular means of transportation in areas surrounded by water, like Venice in Italy.

You can identify a boat when you see a small vehicle on the water carrying a limited number of people. It may have a sail or an engine, depending on what type of boat it is. Some are known for their ability to move with great speed, while others are designed for more laid-back activities.

PARTS OF
A BOAT

Even though the only parts people usually see are the ones above the surface of the water, a boat actually has functioning parts that go way into the water and help the boat work as it should. Some of these important parts are:

Hull: The *hull* is the outer covering of a boat or its body. It gives the boat its shape and the required framework and balance. Some hulls are made with wooden materials, while some are made of steel or aluminum, but the most expensive boats are made with fiberglass or other fancy coatings.

Deck: The *deck* is best described as the inner layer of the boat or, more precisely, the floor. The deck is where sitting platforms are mounted, where people stand, or any other place meant for the passengers.

Sails: Sails are those large pieces of cloth you see on pirate boats or ships. They are attached in a way that allows the wind to push against them, moving the boat in the passengers' preferred direction. It is an important part of some boats that helps them move and determine their speed.

Engine: A watercraft's engine works the way it does in every other vehicle; it produces combustion, causing a burst of power that pushes the boat and causes it to move. You will understand this better as you read on.

Paddle: Paddles are long materials with grips and flat ends, or *blades*, that can be used to manually control the movement of the boat. One or more passengers paddle a boat by digging the flat end into the water and pushing the water in the opposite direction to help produce a forward movement of the boat; similar to the paddles are oars, which have a similar shape but differ slightly.

Types of boats

Sailboats: These are boats with sails that use the wind to help them move.

Motorboats: Motorboats use engines to help them move through the water.

Rowboats: These are small boats that are moved by oars.

Paddleboats: Paddleboats are similar to rowboats, but they're moved by paddles instead of oars.

HOW MOTORBOATS MOVE ON WATER

Motorboats move on the water with the help of *propellers*. A propeller is a set of blades that rotates when attached to a boat's engine. As soon as the engine is powered, it creates a force that heads straight to the propeller and rotates it with great speed. As the propeller rotates, it pushes water backward; as it does this, it generates thrust, a corresponding force that pushes the boat forward. The faster the propeller pushes the water backward, the faster the boat moves forward. As you would guess, the boat stops when the engine is turned off, and there is no propeller to keep pushing the water backward.

Hence, the propeller's shape and size and engine speed work together to determine how fast or slow the boat is. Also, some motorboats use a flat material (wood or metal) called a *rudder* to steer the boat left or right. Rudders are usually attached to the back of boats to help them steer properly.

WHAT ARE BOATS USED FOR?

Depending on the type of boat, people use them for various purposes, including racing, recreation, rescuing, and transportation. Specifically, the police go for their police boats when chasing suspects who are trying to escape through the water. People also use bigger boats to transport goods and other materials.

Did you know?

A boat that can float on the surface of the water and also go below the surface is called a *submarine*. The military uses submarines when trying to sneak into enemy territory without being spotted.

CHAPTER TWENTY-FIVE: TRAINS

Another type of vehicle is the *train*. A train is a long and strong vehicle that moves on special tracks called *rails. It* has the capacity to carry many loads of various materials held in boxes behind the engine compartment. Trains are one of the oldest means of transportation; the world's first steam-powered railway journey took place on the 21st of February, 1804, in South Wales. As other vehicles are designed to move on roads, on the water, or in the air, trains are specially designed to fit on two parallel metal rails fitted to the ground by *ties*. Rails are made of steel, while ties are usually made of concrete or wood. Have you ever noticed that trains mainly travel through *subways* and other designated parts of a city? Subway trains travel through special underground tunnels to ensure that their movement is separated from regular traffic. This is because of how much longer and faster they are than passenger vehicles that drive on roads.

COMPONENTS
OF A TRAIN

Locomotive: The *locomotive* is a very important part of the train. It contains the engine that supplies the power to pull the rest of the train. A locomotive can be powered by steam, diesel, or electricity.

Cars: *Cars* are compartments that carry passengers or cargo. They can also be called "coaches" and "boxcars" and are attached to the locomotive by parts called *couplers*. The design of each car is made to suit the purpose it is meant to serve, either to carry people or *freight* (cargo.)

Tracks: Also known as *railways*, *tracks* are long parallel lines on the ground designed to guide the train and keep it moving in the right direction.

Signals: As their name suggests, signals are used to show the operator or driver of the locomotive when to perform some operations on the train.

Station: Train *stations* are special places where people get on or off a train or where freight is loaded and offloaded from a train. Trains are meant to stop when they get to these designated stations.

TYPES OF TRAINS

Passenger train: A passenger train has cars with seats and compartments for luggage designed for those traveling long distances. It is usually more comfortable, with accessible entrances and exits that people can use at stations.

Freight train: This type of train is specially designed with body parts strong enough to carry heavy cargo. Freight trains do not transport people except the operator or driver and other people working with him or her. Apart from the locomotive, the types of cars attached are determined by the nature of the freight. They could be tanks carrying liquid, boxes carrying food, or open cars carrying animals, minerals, or any other products.

Commuter train: A commuter train is designed to transport people who travel short distances, usually people who live in the suburbs and work in the city. Most commuter trains have specific times they arrive and depart the stations, and their movements can be easily predictable. Most people prefer to use this means of transportation because of its cheap cost compared to buses, and because it produces less pollution and is environmentally friendly.

HOW TRAINS WORK

Have you ever stopped to imagine how a train generates enough power to start moving and pull all the cars attached to one another? Well, it's a simple process, and it solely depends on the form of energy the train is built to use.

- Electric trains require electricity to power themselves, just like your mobile phone needs to be connected to a socket to charge. An electric train is connected to overhead wires or a *third rail* to generate energy that can be converted into motion.
- Diesel trains are trains whose engines are powered by diesel fuel. These engines burn diesel to create the power they require to move.
- Steam trains are powered by steam engines that require heat to create steam and then generate energy.

After any of these trains has generated energy from its source, its wheels convert it into motion. Just like any other vehicle, a train's wheels are connected to its engine by a driveshaft, and the driveshaft is also connected to the wheels. As the engine rolls the driveshaft, it, in turn, rolls the wheels, and the rail or track guides the train as it moves in the right direction.

CHAPTER TWENTY-SIX: ELEVATORS

Unless you're a fitness nut or just want to find out exactly how many steps there are in a tall building, you would likely rather hop in the elevator and float your way up to the top floor.

Hop aboard as we float our way through the history of elevators and how they work so well.

WHAT IS AN ELEVATOR?

An elevator is another type of vehicle that transports people, but in this case, it's from one floor to another, usually inside a building. Some people call it a *lift* because it moves vertically (up and down.) An elevator or lift is usually powered by electricity, which is why people can get stuck when there is a power outage.

The idea of elevators came into existence when people needed to transport themselves or materials vertically to heights they could not reach on their own. It started as a *hoist system*, using pulleys that were manually controlled by manpower or animals. This idea was improved when steam-powered elevators were designed, and today the safest and easiest method is still in use—electricity-powered elevators.

PARTS OF AN ELEVATOR

Car: An elevator car is a compartment that carries people through different floors. It is simply where you are when you say, "I am in the elevator."

Cables: *Cables* are very strong cords made of steel used to pull up and lower cars.

Counterweight: This is a heavy material used for balancing the weight a car is carrying. A counterweight is usually attached to the cable and moves in the opposite direction of a car's movement.

Doors: Most elevator doors are made of strong metal that opens and closes at the edge of each floor to allow easy access and exit.

Hoistway: A *hoistway* is a hollow space in which the car travels up and down. Usually, you don't see the hoistway because an elevator does not have a window, and the doors are always closed during movement for safety reasons.

Machine room: An elevator's *machine room* is a section that houses the elevator's control system and motor. It is typically located on the topmost floor.

Safety devices: Safety devices include a *governor*, a brake, and a *limit switch*; they help prevent an accident or prevent the elevator from falling if the motor fails or cables break. A governor is a sensor that detects the speed of the car and activates the brake to keep the car from falling if it detects that the car is moving too fast. The brake helps the car to stop moving if the motor fails. The brake is also activated by the limit switch once it senses that the car is at the top or bottom of the hoistway.

TYPES OF ELEVATORS AND HOW THEY MOVE

Traction elevator: This is the most common type of elevator. Traction elevators use cables and counterweights to move the car up and down the hoistway. The cables are connected to both the car and the counterweight and are wound around a traction sheave that hangs above the car and counterweight. The traction sheave is connected to an electric motor that powers or turns. As the sheave makes a turn, it either pulls the car up or lowers it down as the counterweight goes the opposite way.

Hydraulic elevator: Hydraulic elevators aren't as common as traction elevators. They work by using a *hydraulic cylinder* filled with oil, which supports the car as it moves up and down through the hoistway. Before the car moves, a pump is used to add pressure to the oil in the cylinder; as it does this, the oil pushes a piston up or down, and the elevator responds by going up or down.

BENEFITS OF ELEVATORS

Convenience: Recently, elevators have become a necessary part of any building with many floors in order to make it convenient for people with mobility issues (who use wheelchairs) to transport themselves conveniently. Typically, elevators are an easy option for people to move from different floors in a building.

Efficiency: Most people want to get to their destinations as quickly as possible. With elevators, everyone can efficiently reduce the time they would spend climbing many stairs and getting tired.

Safety: As explained earlier, elevators have safety devices that keep them from falling. It is a safe way to move between floors without fear or complications; walking on stairs could be dangerous, and people may sometimes slip and fall.

Accessibility: Imagine how accessible your school would be if pupils who need wheelchairs could also use an elevator! It creates an equal environment that includes everyone

Elevators are fun and easy to use, but it's important that you avoid the following:

- Running in and out of the elevator when it has not fully stopped moving
- Exceeding the maximum weight of an elevator

Trying to climb out of a stuck elevator; rather, wait for rescuers to get to you.

CHAPTER TWENTY-SEVEN: BRIDGES

Bridges are structures that help people cross over things, from valleys to rivers and swamps. Before bigger bridges were constructed to help vehicles (cars, buses, and trains), people created various platforms for crossing nature's many obstacles. The earliest forms of bridges were made with stones, pieces of wood, huge logs of wood, and strong ropes, and as the world became more civilized, with the invention of vehicles, bigger bridges made with concrete and iron bars became popular.

TYPES OF BRIDGES

Arch bridges: An *arch bridge* is made of strong beams or concrete to form an arc shape over the gap to support the weight of the bridge. Some arch supports are made to stand on the surface of the bridge, while some go through the bridge to support it from above and below. A popular example of an arch bridge is the Sydney Harbour Bridge in Australia.

Truss bridges: These bridges are made with strong bars that form triangular shapes to support the bridge's weight. An example of a truss bridge is the Forth Bridge in Scotland.

Beam bridges: As the name implies, these are bridges made of strong beams that hold the bridge's weight. Beam bridges are typically not as strong as arch and truss bridges, but they are easier to build. An example of a beam bridge is the Lake Ponchartrain Causeway Bridge in Louisiana.

Suspension bridges: These types are usually made of towers and strong cables, which hang from these towers to carry the weight of the bridge. They are popular options when long-distance bridges are built. An example of a suspension bridge is the Golden Gate Bridge in San Francisco.

Double-decker bridges: Double-decker bridges are strong, built to provide passage for people and vehicles with two layers directly above each other. A double-decker bridge requires more beams and support materials than other bridges, as it is expected to bear

114

more weight. An example of a double-decked bridge is the George Washington Bridge in the United States.

PARTS OF
BRIDGES

You have probably seen a bridge before and may have stuck your head out of the car to look closer. Here are some of the things you must have seen and others that are hidden from you by the top of the bridge:

Abutments: The *abutments* are the parts of the bridge that support the ends of the bridge. These are the parts that link and hold the bridge to the ground's surface. Abutments are usually made of masonry or concrete.

Deck: The deck is the surface of the bridge. This is the part on which people and vehicles move. Decks may be made of steel or concrete, or even wood, depending on the type of bridge.

Piers: These are the vertical pillars that support the bridge's deck. They are built to be strong and heavy enough to carry a certain weight. They may also be made of steel, wood, or concrete, depending on the type of bridge.

Girders: These are the horizontal beams that go directly under the deck to support it as it is laid on the piers. The deck is supported by the girders, and the piers support the girders. They may also be made of different materials, depending on the type of bridge.

Foundation: This is the part of the bridge that goes below the piers. The piers stand on the foundation, while the foundation is made to go through the ground and balance itself to carry the weight of the whole bridge. The foundation is typically made of concrete or masonry; a bridge's foundation to be planted into a body of water is never made of steel, as it can rust and wear away as it reacts to the surrounding water.

CHAPTER TWENTY-EIGHT: SKYSCRAPERS

Have you ever looked at the towering buildings around you and wondered whether they touch the sky? Can they peek above the clouds? *Skyscrapers* are super tall buildings that soar high above the ground level as if they are heading straight for the sky; that's where the name "skyscraper" came from.

Skyscrapers are architectural structures designed and constructed to accommodate more people and things on a small piece of land. Hence, every skyscraper has multiple floors or levels. Because of their great weight and height, they are designed to have strong foundations that go deep into the ground to withstand strong winds and earthquakes, so they are super safe and sturdy. These magnificent constructions are built with long-lasting materials like steel, concrete, and glass, allowing them to withstand pressure and contain various spaces, including offices, residential apartments, hotels, and business headquarters. Skyscrapers are symbols of human progress, displaying advancements in engineering, technology, and design that allow buildings to appear to scrape the sky. The Burj Khalifa in Dubai is currently the tallest skyscraper in the world. It reaches an incredible 2,717 feet above the ground.

Building a skyscraper is no easy task. A talented team of architects, engineers, and builders must collaborate to make it happen. First, they create interesting designs and plans, such as a gigantic blueprint. Construction workers lift the materials up to the necessary floors using cranes and heavy machinery. It's like putting together an enormous puzzle in the sky!

COMPONENTS OF
A SKYSCRAPER

Foundation: The foundation is the skyscraper's base, usually built of concrete or steel, that provides stability and distributes the building's weight to the ground. It must be sturdy enough to support the structure's massive weight. A natural rule for every building is that the taller the building is, the deeper its foundation must go into the ground.

Structural Frame: The structural frame is like the skyscraper's skeleton. It comprises steel or supporting concrete columns, beams, and load-bearing walls. They offer support and uniformly distribute the structure's weight, ensuring stability and strength.

Floors: Skyscrapers have several floors or levels that are vertically stacked. Each floor comprises a mix of concrete slabs, steel beams, and other components. Each floor can accommodate a variety of uses, including offices, housing, and commercial areas.

Elevators and Stairs: Given their height, skyscrapers rely on elevators to carry passengers between floors. Staircases are also necessary for emergencies or when people prefer to take the steps rather than the elevator.

Façade: The *façade* is the skyscraper's external face or outer shell. It is made of various materials, including glass, steel, aluminum, and stone. The façade beautifies the skyscraper, provides weather protection, and allows natural light into the building.

Mechanical Systems: Skyscrapers require a variety of automated systems to provide comfortable and functional areas. Heating, ventilation, and air conditioning (HVAC) systems regulate temperature and humidity, plumbing systems feed and drain water, and electrical systems illuminate and power the building.

Safety Systems: Skyscrapers incorporate various safety features, such as fire suppression systems, smoke detectors, sprinklers, and emergency exits. These systems are crucial for the safety and well-being of occupants in emergencies.

Rooftop: A skyscraper's rooftop can be used for a variety of purposes. Some skyscrapers include helipads for emergency incidents or air transportation, while others have rooftop gardens or observation decks where occupants and tourists can enjoy panoramic city views.

Skyscrapers are more than just tall structures; they are feats of human invention and imagination. They represent the amazing things that individuals can do when they work together. Humans value skyscrapers because they provide space for living, working, and recreational activities in densely populated places. They maximize land use, provide housing for many people, provide stunning views, boost economic growth, and contribute to urban development and sustainability.

Skyscrapers are helpful to humans, but as the adage goes, there are two sides to every coin; therefore, here are a few downsides of skyscrapers.

High Construction and Maintenance Costs: Constructing and maintaining skyscrapers can be extremely expensive due to the specialized materials, equipment, and expertise required. Building and maintaining such tall structures can be a significant financial burden.

Environmental Impact: Skyscrapers consume large amounts of energy for heating, cooling, lighting, and other operations. This energy consumption contributes to carbon emissions and can harm the environment if not managed sustainably.

Strain on infrastructure: Skyscrapers require robust infrastructure to support their operations, including transportation, water supply, waste management, and emergency services. The increased demand for these tall structures can strain existing infrastructure systems.

CHAPTER TWENTY-NINE: ROAD SIGNS AND CONSTRUCTION SIGNS

Road signs are those colorful shapes and signs along the road that convey special messages, but they aren't just random symbols or pictures; they're important tools that guide people's movement as they drive to keep them safe. These signs ensure smooth and secure transportation and contain all kinds of information, from cautionary warnings to helpful directions. So, buckle up and get ready to explore the language of the road and construction signs surrounding you daily!

Road signs are important visual markers along roadways that are designed with specific symbols, colors, and shapes to convey messages quickly and effectively. Road signs communicate various types of information, such as speed limits, directions, hazards, traffic rules, and regulations. They ensure road safety and promote orderly and efficient traffic flow.

Construction signs are temporary signs placed in zones or areas where road work or construction is taking place. These signs warn drivers and pedestrians about the presence of construction work, potential hazards, and necessary changes to traffic patterns. Construction signs provide essential guidance, warnings, and regulatory information, helping to keep drivers and workers safe and facilitating smooth traffic flow around construction sites. They often include messages related to detours, lane closures, reduced speed limits, and other temporary changes in road conditions.

Road signs point you in the proper path, like helpful arrows. Stop signs, yield signs, and one-way signs are a few of the many signs you may see beside the road. Here are some more types of road signs you will commonly find.

TYPES OF ROAD SIGNS

Regulatory signs: These signs inform drivers about traffic rules and regulations. They include signs such as:

Stop signs: These signs are red and shaped like an octagon. When you see one, it means you must come to a complete stop and check for any other cars or people before proceeding.

Yield signs: These signs can be triangular and red and white or yellow and shaped like a diamond. They remind drivers to slow down and let other traffic go first if necessary.

One-way signs: These signs are rectangular and have an arrow pointing in a specific direction. They show you that you can only travel in one direction on that particular road.

Speed Limit signs: These signs display the maximum speed allowed on a particular road.

Warning Signs: These are signs used to alert drivers of potential dangers on the road. They are usually yellow and diamond-shaped but can come in a variety of shapes.

Curve Ahead signs: Notify drivers of upcoming bends or curves in the road.

Deer Crossing signs: Warn drivers of areas where deer are known to cross the road.

School Zone signs: Indicate areas near schools where drivers should be cautious due to children present.

Guide signs provide information and directions to help drivers navigate and reach their destinations. They are usually green or blue, with white lettering.

Route signs: Indicate the number or name of a highway or road.

Exit signs: Provide information about upcoming exits on highways.

Destination signs: Display the names of towns, cities, or specific locations along the route.

Construction signs are temporary signs placed in areas undergoing roadwork or construction.

Road Work Ahead signs: This sign warns drivers that they should anticipate roadwork and adjust their driving accordingly. The sign is an orange diamond-shaped sign with a black symbol depicting a figure of a worker holding a shovel or a flag.

Detour signs: The symbol used for the detour is a rectangular sign with a black symbol on a yellow background. The symbol typically consists of an arrow pointing in a specific direction, indicating an alternative route to bypass a road closure or construction area.

Lane Closure signs: Indicate that certain lanes are closed and drivers should merge accordingly.

Information signs offer additional information to drivers, such as services and amenities available along the road.

Gas Station signs: Indicate the presence and location of nearby fuel stations.

Rest Area signs: Inform drivers of rest areas where they can take breaks and use facilities.

Hospital signs: Provide directions to nearby hospitals or medical facilities.

These are just a few examples of road signs you will encounter while traveling. It is important to familiarize yourself with these signs and their meanings to understand why your parents or driver makes certain decisions on the road.

Road and construction signs are like guardians of the streets, ensuring your safety while traveling. They help you know where to go, when to stop, and how to avoid potential dangers. Always remember to pay attention to these signs and follow their instructions. They are there to ensure you have fun and safe journeys every time you hit the road.

CHAPTER THIRTY:
CRANES

These huge machines are the most noticeable parts of any construction project, towering above the site and tirelessly lifting and moving massive objects with unmatched precision and strength. The crane, an engineering marvel that has become the backbone of the modern world, makes the construction world go round.

In this chapter, we will lift high up into the world of cranes, exploring their astounding powers, numerous varieties, and their crucial role in shaping urban environments. These giants have altered how humans create, transport, and transform their surroundings, from the tallest tower cranes decorating city skylines to mobile cranes efficiently navigating construction sites.

WHAT IS A CRANE?

A crane is a gigantic machine with a long arm called a boom. It can be as tall as a skyscraper, with cables, chains, or ropes to lift and move heavy loads. Cranes come in different shapes and sizes, but they all have one thing in common: they are incredibly powerful. Cranes have a wide range of uses and play a vital role in various activities. Here are a few of them:

Construction sites: Cranes are essential in building skyscrapers, houses, bridges, and other structures. They lift heavy materials like steel beams, concrete blocks, and even prefabricated walls to help build these impressive creations.

Shipping and ports: Look out for cranes next time you pass by a busy port. They are used to load and unload cargo from ships. Cranes carefully lift containers, cars, and other goods from the ship's deck or the shore, making it possible for people to enjoy products worldwide.

Rescue operations: Cranes can also be superheroes in emergencies. During disasters like earthquakes or accidents, cranes help lift debris and heavy objects, allowing rescue workers to reach people who may be trapped and need help.

Film sets and events: Have you ever watched a movie or attended a big event? Cranes are sometimes used to set up stages, lighting, and cameras. They can even lift actors or performers high up to create exciting and dramatic scenes.

BENEFITS OF CRANES

Cranes benefit humans in different ways; some of them are:

Efficiency: Cranes make construction projects go faster and more efficiently. They can lift and move heavy materials much quicker than if humans did it manually. This means buildings can be constructed faster, saving time and resources.

Safety: By using cranes, workers can avoid lifting heavy objects by hand, reducing the risk of injuries and accidents. Cranes are designed to handle heavy loads safely and efficiently, ensuring a safer working environment.

Precision: Some cranes are designed to be incredibly precise machines. They can lift objects accurately, placing them exactly where they need to be. This precision is crucial in construction, as it helps ensure structures are built correctly and in the right position.

Innovation: Cranes represent the amazing power of human innovation and engineering. The technology and design behind cranes continue to evolve, leading to even more advanced machines that can perform incredible tasks.

DISADVANTAGES OF CRANES

While cranes are undoubtedly powerful and essential machines in various industries, they have some potential downsides that must be taken into consideration. Here are a few of them:

Safety risks: Operating cranes involves inherent risks for the operators and those working near them. Accidents can occur due to equipment failure, improper use, human error, or inadequate training. It is crucial to put safety measures in place, provide comprehensive training, and adhere to strict protocols to mitigate these risks.

Environmental impact: The operation of cranes, particularly larger models, can have environmental consequences. They consume energy, often relying on diesel fuel or electricity, contributing to carbon emissions and air pollution. Additionally, the construction of large-scale projects may result in habitat disruption, deforestation, or other ecological impacts. Implementing sustainable practices, exploring cleaner alternatives, and minimizing environmental footprint wherever possible is important.

Noise and disruption: Cranes can make a lot of noise when working, especially when lifting huge objects or using many cranes on a construction site. This noise can bother nearby residents, businesses, and wildlife habitats. Noise pollution can be reduced through suitable scheduling, adopting noise-reducing measures, and creating noise barriers.

Space requirements: Cranes, particularly tower cranes, require large installation and operation space. This might be difficult in densely populated urban areas when space is limited. Space limits can be addressed by coordinating with city planning authorities, optimizing crane positioning, and evaluating other lifting methods.

Traffic and logistical considerations: Cranes on building sites or in metropolitan areas can disrupt traffic flow, pedestrian safety, and overall project logistics. Proper traffic management strategies, coordination with local authorities, and clear communication with stakeholders are required to avoid delays and guarantee smooth operations.

CHAPTER THIRTY-ONE: FORKLIFTS

A *forklift* is like a mechanical workhorse. It works extremely hard and helps workers to be more efficient. Forklifts are found in warehouses, backrooms of supermarkets and furniture stores, and in many other industrial areas. A forklift is a small but mighty machine with a strong metal two-pronged "fork" at the front. It is powered by batteries or fuel and has special controls that allow the operator to lift and lower the fork, making it easier to move heavy objects.

Here are some of the most common uses of a forklift:

Warehouses: Forklifts are like busy bees in warehouses, where they help move goods and materials. They can lift heavy pallets of products and place them on high shelves or transport them from one area to another. Forklifts are essential for efficiently storing and retrieving items in large warehouses.

Factories: In factories, forklifts transport raw materials, such as metal or plastic, to different workstations. They can lift heavy machine parts, tools, and finished products, ensuring that everything is in the right place at the right time. Forklifts help keep the production process running smoothly.

Construction sites: When buildings are being constructed or renovated, forklifts lend a helping hand. They move heavy construction materials like bricks, cement bags, and steel beams, making it easier for workers to access what they need and keeping the site organized.

Retail and stores: Next time you visit a big store, take a look around. Forklifts might be quietly working behind the scenes to restock shelves with products or transport items from the storage area to the sales floor. They help keep stores well-stocked and ensure that products are readily available for customers.

TYPES OF FORKLIFTS

Several types of forklifts are available, each designed to cater to specific material handling needs and work environments. Here are some common types of forklifts:

Counterbalance forklifts: These are the most widely used forklifts, designed with a weight at the rear to counterbalance the lifted load. They come with various power options, like electric, gas, or diesel, and are suitable for indoor and outdoor applications.

Reach trucks: Reach trucks are ideal for narrow aisles and high stacking. They have extending forks that can reach into racking systems, enabling operators to access loads at height with precision.

Order pickers: Order pickers are designed for picking individual items from shelves or racks. They typically have an elevated platform that allows operators to access items at different levels, increasing efficiency.

Pallet jacks: Also known as pallet trucks or pump trucks, pallet jacks are used for moving palletized loads horizontally. They do not have an extending mast and can be manually operated or powered.

Side loader Forklifts: Because they can lift items from the side, side loader forklifts are ideal for handling long or wide loads such as timber, pipes, or sheets of material. They are widely utilized in the woodworking, metal manufacturing, and construction industries.

Rough terrain forklifts: These forklifts are built for outdoor use on rough or uneven surfaces. They are equipped with larger, more rugged tires and have higher ground clearance to navigate challenging terrains, making them suitable for construction sites or agricultural settings.

Industrial Reach Stackers: Reach stackers are heavy-duty forklifts used in shipping ports, warehouses, and logistics centers. They are designed for stacking and handling shipping containers or heavy loads with exceptional stability and lifting capacities.

These are just a few examples of the diverse range of available forklift types, each with specific features and applications. The choice of forklift depends on factors such as load capacity, maneuverability requirements, operating environment, and the nature of the materials being handled.

WHY FORKLIFTS
ARE IMPORTANT

Efficiency: Forklifts make tasks quicker and more efficient. They can move heavy objects that would otherwise be challenging for humans to carry. With forklifts, items can be lifted, transported, and stored efficiently, saving time and effort.

Safety: Forklifts are designed to handle heavy loads in a controlled and safe manner. Workers can avoid straining their muscles or risking injury while moving heavy objects using forklifts. Forklifts help create a safer working environment.

Precision: Forklifts are precise machines. Operators can maneuver them in tight spaces, aligning the forks to accurately pick up and place objects. This precision ensures that items are moved safely and avoids accidental damage.

Versatility: Forklifts come with different attachments, such as clamps or platforms, that allow them to handle various types of loads. This versatility enables forklifts to adapt to different tasks and makes them a valuable tool in various industries.

Don't forget, though you may not know when one is coming; they are easily identifiable once you've found one. It's really all in the name — each forklift has a fork-shaped carrier in the front! Chances are, you've seen one before, but if you didn't already know what the heck it was, now you know it's quite simple — it's a huge, mobile "fork" that "lifts"!

CHAPTER THIRTY-TWO: RECYCLING

Recycling has become a powerful tool to help us safeguard the earth and create a more beautiful future where the Earth is as green, clean, and pristine as it can be. Recycling is definitely more than just a buzzword; it is a solution that enables individuals and communities to make a positive difference. We will dive into recycling in all its depth in this chapter. We'll take a look at its significance, benefits, and some practical ways for everyone to become involved. Prepare to learn the secrets of the green revolution and how recycling can change your environment for the better.

WHAT IS RECYCLING?

Recycling is the process of collecting, sorting, and transforming waste materials into new products. Instead of throwing things away, you give them a second chance by converting them into something different. This helps reduce the amount of waste in landfills and saves valuable resources.

BENEFITS OF RECYCLING

Saving resources: When you recycle materials like paper, plastic, glass, and metal, you can use them to make new products. This means you do not have to extract and use as many raw materials from the earth. By doing this, you are conserving precious resources like trees, oil, and minerals.

Reducing pollution: Recycling helps to reduce pollution in your environment. By recycling, you can reduce the amount of waste burned or buried in landfills, preventing harmful gasses and chemicals from being released into the air, water, and soil.

Energy conservation: Making products from recycled materials often requires less energy than using raw materials. By recycling, we save energy, which helps reduce greenhouse gas emissions and combat climate change.

Job creation and economic benefits: recycling and the associated industries create employment opportunities. From collecting and sorting recyclables to processing and manufacturing recycled products, recycling supports many jobs in local communities. Also, recycling can stimulate economic growth by promoting the development of a circular economy and reducing dependence on costly imports of raw materials.

Cleaner communities: Recycling helps keep your neighborhoods clean and beautiful. When you recycle, less litter and waste clutters your streets and parks.

Empowerment: Recycling can give you a sense of pride and empowerment, knowing you are actively making a difference in the world. It can empower you to be responsible stewards of the earth and inspire others to follow your lead.

Recycling is a way for everyone to pitch in and help make the Earth a bit more beautiful and healthy . . . and it's probably a lot easier than you think.

GET INVOLVED

Want to help your community and preserve the environment? Here are some simple steps to get started:

Learn what can be recycled: Find out what materials your community recycles. Common items include paper, cardboard, plastic bottles, aluminum cans, glass bottles, and certain types of metal.

Separate and sort: Set up recycling bins at home, labeled for different materials. Rinse containers and remove non-recyclable parts like plastic lids or food residue. Sort the items into the appropriate bins.

Follow local guidelines: Check with your local recycling center or waste management facility to learn about specific guidelines in your area. They can provide information on collection schedules, drop-off locations, and any special instructions.

Spread the word: Share your knowledge with family and friends. Encourage them to recycle too. Engage in discussions with your loved ones about the importance of recycling and its positive effects on the environment. Highlight the benefits, such as conserving energy, reducing greenhouse gas emissions, and protecting wildlife habitats. Consider hosting recycling awareness events or workshops for your family and friends, where you ask adults who are big on recycling to educate you. These gatherings can involve educational presentations, interactive activities, and practical demonstrations to showcase the impact of recycling and provide guidance on how to recycle properly.

Recycling is more than just a simple act of separating materials into different bins. It is a potentially powerful thing that can empower people to start treating the world around them with a bit more care and love. Through recycling, you help to conserve precious natural resources, reduce landfill waste, save energy, prevent pollution, and protect our planet's beauty.

Some items that can be made from recycled materials are:

- Paper, cardboard, and paperboard can be recycled into new paper products, such as notebooks, folders, envelopes, and toilet paper.

- Plastic bottles, containers, and bags can be recycled into new plastic products, such as toys, furniture, and park benches.

- Glass bottles and jars can be recycled into new glass products, such as windows, bottles, and tableware.

- Metal cans, aluminum foil, and wire can be recycled into new metal products, such as cars, appliances, and jewelry.

- Tires, shoes, and other rubber products can be recycled into new rubber products, such as playground equipment and mats.

We could tell you that "you should pledge to recycle diligently," "you should educate others about its importance," and "advocate for improved recycling infrastructure." But, somehow, it seems that every "should" falls flat and sounds a little condescending. With recycling, as with most other things, it's not so much about *needing* to do it as it is about your *intentions* and *how* you do it. And, as with anything, it's always best to have some fun with it and remember not to take things too seriously; don't start yelling at your neighbors because they don't use the recycling bin! The best we can say is this: our planet, with all of its amazing wildlife and unique humans, is certainly worth a little love.

CONCLUSION

If you have journeyed this far, you're surely filled to the brim with fantastic ideas and visions of how things work! At the very least, you've gotten your feet wet and satisfied the beginnings of your curiosity about the what, why, how, and when of the things you see and use around you.

Those of you particularly curious characters out there who followed along closely are well-equipped with a whole basket of practical knowledge, from how an elevator works, why a ship doesn't sink but a car does, how engineers lift heavy materials to the top of skyscrapers, to why helicopters are used for some things instead of airplanes.

The great men and women who invented these things had great minds, and they put them to great use, imagining brand-new tools and ways of doing things. **HOW THINGS WORK** is designed to open up brand new vistas of thought and to allow your mind to roam free and think creatively. Who knows? You just may shine that creative spark so brightly that you yourself end up in a book very much like this one! Now that you've learned some new things, it's ok to brag a little. Go ahead; feel free to share a few facts with friends and family. Even if they yawn with boredom or merely *act* like they're interested, you've certainly earned the right to spread a little information. As always, just make sure that it's all in good fun (it's definitely best to resist the understandable urge to push and shove your little sibling if they stick out their tongue at your newfound knowledge!) Regardless of how folks react, you'll be a step ahead—sharing knowledge is a surefire way to seal it within your brain; even if nobody seems to care, you surely won't forget *how things work*.